HANDBOOK
of
TORAH
and
MENTAL
HEALTH

MOSAICA PRESS

HANDBOOK
of
TORAH
and
MENTAL
HEALTH

DAVID H. ROSMARIN, PHD, ABPP
RABBI SAUL HAIMOFF, PSYD

Copyright © 2019 by Mosaica Press

ISBN-10: 1-946351-84-9
ISBN-13: 978-1-946351-84-5

All rights reserved. No part of this book may be used or reproduced or transmitted in any form or by any means, electronic or mechanical, including photocopying, recording, or by any information storage and retrieval system, without written permission from the publisher.

Published by Mosaica Press, Inc.
www.mosaicapress.com
info@mosaicapress.com

לע"נ יהושע רפאל פולונסקי

IN LOVING MEMORY OF

YEHOSHUA "SHUA" POLONSKY, PSYD

A DEDICATED FRIEND AND COLLEAGUE
AND A TRUE TORAH PSYCHOLOGIST

Rabbi Dovid Cohen
1518 East 7th Street, Brooklyn NY, 11230

---

17 Shevat, 5779

I have read the preface and have perused various subjects dealt with in the *Handbook of Torah and Mental Health*. I write "perused," but I must admit that it was difficult for me to stop reading. However, I was certain that the authors did not want me to become addicted.

The material dealt with fulfills the needs of those desirous to imbibe from the wellsprings of Torah. On the other hand, a librarian will be perplexed under which topic to classify this *sefer*, since Torah titans termed psychology as *Toras Ha'adam* (the knowledge of mankind), which embraces all the universal challenges that mankind is confronted with.

I bless the authors with that blessing which is given to voyagers, since it is their plan to embark on many thrilling voyages. May you be successful in your endeavors to return with many beautiful gifts for your readers.

With warmth, love, and admiration,

Dovid Cohen

David Pelcovitz, PhD
Straus Chair in Psychology and Education
Yeshiva University

June 19th, 2019

In the *Handbook of Torah and Mental Health,* Dr. David H. Rosmarin and Rabbi Dr. Saul Haimoff address an important gap in the literature on Jewish thinking and clinical psychology. The integration of the timeless wisdom of the Torah with current advances in psychotherapy leads to potent practical insights into the process of change and growth. In this book, the authors do a masterful job in succinctly sharing Torah insights regarding a wide-ranging array of psychological issues—from anxiety and depression to parenting and psychotherapy.

As one of the leading researchers and clinicians in the field of psychology and religion, Dr. Rosmarin writes with clarity and precision. I found myself learning something new on every page as my eyes were opened by his creative approach, which is often informed by his own groundbreaking research on the psychology of religion and spirituality.

I strongly recommend this book to anybody seeking a better understanding of how to address life's inevitable challenges guided by Torah's powerful wisdom integrated with the practical approaches of psychology.

David Pelcovitz

David J. Lieberman, PhD
Noted Psychotherapist, Speaker and Author

July 27th, 2019

The *Handbook of Torah and Mental Health* is highly engaging and equally fascinating—with strong appeal to both layman and scholar alike. Dr. David H. Rosmarin and Rabbi Dr. Saul Haimoff weave together Torah insights with psychological principles that will enrich the reader with a deeper understanding and appreciation for the depth and beauty of Torah wisdom. This is the book that I would have loved to have written, if I had the authors' talent, intellect and insight.

The *Handbook of Torah and Mental Health* deserves wide readership. I wish the authors much success with this book and in all of their amazing endeavors.

With respect and warmth,

David Lieberman

TABLE OF CONTENTS

Foreword XV
Introduction 1

Chapter 1
COGNITIVE BEHAVIORAL THERAPY

1. Our Behaviors Impact How We Feel 7
2. Consistency: The Key to Establishing Good Habits 8
3. Monitoring Progress Increases
   Your Chances of Success 10
4. How Emotional Reasoning Distorts Our Thinking 12
5. Positive Language Can Help Improve Your Attitude ... 14
6. Mind over Matter: How Positive Thinking
   Changes You 15
7. Cognitive Reframing Helps Us Overcome Adversity ... 17
8. Cognitive Distortions Lead to Poor Choices 19
9. Action Begets Learning: The Importance
   of Behavior Change in Psychotherapy 21

10. Tefillin and Cognitive Dissonance:
    Syncing Beliefs and Behaviors 23
11. Teshuvah Gemurah and Relapse Prevention:
    Practice Makes Perfect 24

Chapter 2
DIALECTICAL BEHAVIOR THERAPY

1. Opposite Action Can Change Your Emotions 27
2. Validating the Emotional Pain of Self-Injury 29
3. Wise Mind: The Harmonious Balance
   of Emotion and Intellect 31
4. Mindfulness and the Menorah:
   The Calming Candle Meditation 32
5. Using Dialectical Thinking
   to Balance Contradictory Emotions 34
6. Sitting with Willing and Open Hands
   Creates Acceptance...............................36
7. Making Time for Mindfulness to Find Peace of Mind ..38
8. Patience Is the Ability to Tolerate Suffering 39

Chapter 3
GENERAL PSYCHOTHERAPY

1. Unconditional Positive Regard......................42
2. The Talking Cure: How Psychotherapy Can Help 43
3. The Influence of Subconscious Forces 45

4. Projecting Our Flaws onto Others....................48

5. Maslow's Pyramid and Jacob's Ladder:
   Fulfilling a Hierarchy of Needs......................49

Chapter 4
ANXIETY AND OBSESSIVE-COMPULSIVE DISORDER

1. Real Concerns vs. Obsessive Worries 52

2. Taking Deep Breaths to Cope with Anxiety 54

3. Setting Aside "Worry Time" Each Day to Fight Anxiety..55

4. The Approach-Avoidance Conflict:
   Lean In to Your Anxieties 57

5. Doubt, Uncertainty, and Choice Overload 59

6. Chronic Anxiety Can Cause Physical Health Problems..60

7. Trust in God Can Help with Worry 62

Chapter 5
DEPRESSION

1. Scheduling Pleasant Activities
   to Help with Depression 65

2. The Cyclical Nature of Depression...................67

3. Passive Suicidal Ideation:
   Coping with Serious Emotional Pain................68

4. Religious Practice without Belief
   Can Worsen Depression 70

5. Finding Meaning Helps Overcome Grief 71

XII *Handbook of Torah and Mental Health*

Chapter 6
PARENTING

1. A Unified Voice in the Home
   Improves Child Behaviors.........................73
2. A Healthy Marriage Promotes Children's
   Spiritual Development 75
3. The Rambam's Token Economy:
   Rewarding Children with Prizes...................77
4. Breaking Out of the Coercive Cycle in Parenting......79
5. Effective Parenting Begins with Reducing Commands..81
6. Bedtime Routines Improve Sleep 82
7. Corporal Punishment Is Poor Modeling
   and Emotionally Damaging to Children.............84
8. Authoritative Parenting Style:
   Blending Chessed and Gevurah Makes Tiferes 86
9. Education Is a Preparation for Life 89

Chapter 7
SPIRITUALITY AND MENTAL HEALTH

1. A Torah Perspective on Tragedy
   Helps to Find Value in Suffering 91
2. Going to Synagogue May Lead
   to a Longer, Healthier Life 93

3. Practicing Gratitude Improves Happiness,
   Satisfaction, and More..........................95
4. Change Your Nature through Daily Practice..........97
5. Taking It One Step at a Time to Change Your Life.....98
6. Hardship Can Increase Our Willpower.............100
7. The Ability to Delay Gratification
   Leads to a Better Life.........................101
8. Noticing Changes in Our Environment............103
9. Guided Imagery and Visualizations Can Help Us
   Fulfill Our Potential..........................105
10. Character Change Is the Greatest
    Human Achievement.........................107
11. The Ultimate Cure for Improving One's Character..108

FOREWORD

For more than three millennia, the Jewish People dedicated themselves to the mission of guarding the Divine prescription for creating a better person and a better world. Protecting that tradition became a national obsession, an act of *diligere Deum*—loving their God, by cherishing His word.

Jewish Sages protected the Sinaitic prescription from adulteration by forbidding its transcription. They only committed major themes and selected details to writing in the dozens of cryptic volumes of the Talmud, Midrash, and Zohar. These repositories were therefore decipherable only with the assistance of a mentor already fluent in the tradition. Parents taught their children, and teachers taught their students, reading these works aloud and clarifying the secrets between the lines—secrets they had heard from their parents and teachers a generation earlier.

Because their tradition stressed psychological health as a prerequisite to spiritual perfection, it contained a comprehensive therapeutic theory and program. But the Torah concealed this high-definition portrait of the human psyche's anatomy, instructions for maintaining psychological health, and prescriptions for recovery from psychopathology. None of this wisdom could be accessed just by reading a scroll; a living guide was always necessary. For more than two thousand years, it seemed that no one was inconvenienced by the mechanism put in place to protect the Jewish tradition. Religiously affiliated Jews had uninhibited access to the Torah's psychological insights, and no one else appeared to be interested.

However, as the frequency and intensity of modern psychopathology soars, so has the West's humble and broad-minded interest in foreign solutions. Today, tenured professors unabashedly borrow empirically verifiable insights and practices from other cultures, and most psychology graduate students get at least some exposure to these imports. But researchers remain frustrated at their inability to independently crack the code of the Jewish oral tradition. The Torah's formula for creating and maintaining psychological health remains about as much of a mystery to outsiders as it has since the Jews first departed Mount Sinai.

In this way, the present contribution is a watershed moment for modern psychology. Dr. Rosmarin is as fluent in the worlds of ancient Israel and Babylonia as he is with the halls of Harvard Psychiatry. He is the perfect emissary and translator, having spent decades in dialogue with carriers of the Jewish oral tradition and mined them for theoretical and practical insights they received from the previous generation's scholars. In his research, he has not only codified these discoveries, but, uniquely, he has tested them, applying Torah psychology in private practice and laboratory studies (see chapter 4, entry 7 of this text). His astounding results testify as much to the system's value as they do to his grasp of it.

This volume is only a teaser. The authors seem to be testing our interest by only presenting a few dozen concepts. I hope that the present volume is met with the enthusiasm it deserves, and that the authors respond with a more comprehensive presentation in the near future.

With deep respect and affection,

Lawrence Kelemen

INTRODUCTION

Historically speaking, the mental health disciplines have maintained a negative attitude toward religion. The origins of this tension can be traced back to the influential works of Sigmund Freud, who called religion a "neurosis,"[1] denigrated the spiritual domain as "patently infantile,"[2] and virulently lambasted his closest colleague, Carl Jung, for appreciating the sacred.[3] More recently, however, psychologists have developed a more receptive attitude toward spirituality and its potential relevance to emotional well-being. This change has arisen from substantial evidence indicating that religious life can impart a positive influence on mental health. It is now widely recognized that religious belief and practice can facilitate emotional wellness, resilience, and lower

---

1   S. Freud, *The Future of an Illusion* (London: Hogarth Press, 1927).
2   S. Freud, *Civilization and Its Discontents* (London: Hogarth Press, 1930).
3   M. Palmer, *Freud and Jung on Religion*, 1st ed. (Abingdon: Routledge, 1997).

incidence and severity of mental health disorders.[4] In fact, for well over two decades, the mental health sciences have embraced and applied methods involving spiritual practice in treatment.[5]

The vast majority of research on the relationship between spirituality and mental health has been conducted outside of Judaism. As such, there remains a lack of appreciation for Torah as a source of psychological wisdom, even though Jews are proportionately far greater in number and influence in the mental health sciences relative to population size. Consider that Jews represent just 0.2% of the world population,[6] yet a preponderance of prominent leaders in the field have been Jewish, including Sigmund Freud, Viktor Frankl, Alfred Adler, Erich Fromm, Stanley Abraham Maslow, Aaron T. Beck, Albert Ellis, and Martin Seligman. In fact, in the 1930s, psychoanalysis was derisively referred to as the "Jewish Science" in European academic circles.[7]

---

4 S. R. Weber and K. I. Pargament, "The role of religion and spirituality in mental health," *Current Opinion in Psychiatry* 27(5) (2014): 358–363.

5 S. Dimidjian and M. M. Linehan, "Defining an agenda for future research on the clinical application of mindfulness practice," *Clinical Psychology: Science and Practice*, 10(2) (2003): 166–171.

6 S. DellaPergola, "World Jewish Population, 2017," in A. Dashefsky and I. Sheskin (Ed.), *American Jewish Year Book*, Vol. 117 (Cham: Springer, 2018).

7 S. Frosh, *Hate and the 'Jewish Science': Anti-Semitism, Nazism and Psychoanalysis* (London: Palgrave Macmillan, 2005), pp. 63–90.

In this regard, it is ironic that Judaism is largely ignored by the field. In other ways, though, the lack of appreciation for Torah wisdom is tragic, since the Torah is replete with insight into human psychology, and it remains an underappreciated and underutilized resource.

In fact, the Torah's teachings are significantly relevant in all matters of mental and emotional welfare, such as depression, anxiety, anger, marriage issues, child-rearing challenges, and many others.

Few—if any other—religions offer such comprehensive guidance as Judaism, which can imbue its adherents' lives with beauty and meaning. Thus, Torah-observant individuals are at an advantage when it comes to psychological well-being; often, it only takes a reminder of the wellspring of insights provided by their faith to initiate the healing process. However, even among groups of traditional and Orthodox Jewish mental health practitioners, Torah wisdom is often marginalized, and is seldom viewed as a worthy guide of psychotherapeutic practice.

With a large majority of the world's population espousing religious practice, spirituality should seemingly serve as a primary locus of mental health and treatment. Despite the negative bias toward religion that has long persisted in the mental health world, current trends offer hope that interest in the relevance of spirituality and religion among psychologists is on the rise. An increasing number of psychologists have begun to recognize the aspects of religion that positively influence mental health, including pro-sociality, acceptance, and resistance to maladaptive thought processes. Fundamentally, religion can offer a sense of meaning in life that cannot be matched by secular approaches alone. We hope that trends toward integration of mental health disciplines and religious practice continue to the benefit of patients.

While empirical research on the relationship between Judaism and mental well-being is still in its infancy,[8] this book seeks to demonstrate that there is already ample evidence indicating the inherent psychological wisdom in Torah. We hope that our work will highlight this not only for the general public, but also for Torah-observant mental health professionals, so that they can better utilize Jewish wisdom in their treatments.

To these ends, we are delighted to present to you this brief text, entitled *Handbook of Torah and Mental Health*. It includes a collection of fifty-six Torah sources that are relevant to mental health. Specific topics span the gamut of mental disorders (e.g., depression, anxiety, obsessions/compulsions) as well as marital and family issues, childrearing and educational matters, and ways to promote emotional wellness, thriving, and happiness. Sources have been collected from the breadth of Jewish written thought spanning a period of

---

[8] https://link.springer.com/chapter/10.1007/978-3-319-21933-2_7.

greater than three thousand years, including *Chumash* (Five Books of Moses), *Nach* (nineteen additional books of the Jewish cannon), *Talmud* (codification of the Oral Torah tradition), *Rishonim* (written commentaries of the Sages through the sixteenth century), and *Acharonim* (contemporary commentaries from the seventeenth century through the modern day). Each entry contains both an original quoted text, an English translation that has been specially prepared for this volume, and a brief description of how the quotation is relevant to one or more mental health issues. Throughout the text, care was taken to include entries whose insights have been validated by clinical science and/or are consistent with current evidence-based psychotherapy practice.

In constructing this text, a crowd-sourcing approach was utilized to identify appropriate Torah sources for inclusion. An email was drafted and syndicated to rabbis and other Jewish community leaders from around the world, soliciting suggestions and recommendations for Torah sources relevant to mental health. We are deeply grateful for the many responses received and the outpouring of support this project has garnered from the international Jewish community. We are also most grateful to our religious mentors, Rabbi Leib Kelemen (Jerusalem, Israel), Rabbi Naftoly Bier (Boston, MA), Rabbi Dovid Cohen (Brooklyn, NY), and Rabbi Sholom Kamenetsky (Philadelphia, PA) for their ongoing guidance, insights, and assistance in shaping this text. Closer to home, we are thankful to our wives and children—in fact, Miri Rosmarin deserves credit for conceiving the idea for this book in the first place. And finally, we are most grateful to God for providing us with the opportunity to highlight some gleanings of Divine mental health wisdom, for a world that is in great need.

David H. Rosmarin and Saul Haimoff
June 2019

Chapter 1

COGNITIVE
BEHAVIORAL
THERAPY

1. OUR BEHAVIORS IMPACT HOW WE FEEL

דע כי האדם נפעל כפי פעולותיו ולבו וכל מחשבותיו תמיד אחר מעשיו שהוא עוסק בהם אם טוב ואם רע...כי אחרי הפעולות נמשכים הלבבות.

Know, that we are directly affected by our behaviors. Our hearts and thoughts always follow after the actions that we do, whether good or bad...for the heart is drawn after behavior.

Sefer Hachinuch, Parashas Bo, mitzvah 16

Most people believe that they behave in accordance with how they feel. However, in this famous excerpt, the *Sefer Hachinuch* teaches us that the opposite is also true: counterintuitively, our thoughts and emotions are directly impacted by the way in which we behave. A substantial body of clinical psychological science has highlighted this as a basic truth of human psychology. For example, facing one's fear is the best way to overcome anxiety,[1] and engaging in positive behaviors is a tried-and-tested method for overcoming depression.[2] In fact, in one famous experiment, participants who held a pen between their teeth (creating a facial expression of smiling) while watching cartoons rated them as more humorous than a control group of individuals who simply watched the cartoons.[3] So, even a basic physical act can lead to changes in the way we think and feel.

2. CONSISTENCY: THE KEY TO ESTABLISHING GOOD HABITS

והמרגיל את עצמו בדרך הזה ארבע או חמש פעמים, לא יכבד עליו אחר כך.

---

[1] L. D. Seligman and T. H. Ollendick, "Cognitive-Behavioral Therapy for Anxiety Disorders in Youth," *Child and Adolescent Psychiatric Clinics of North America* 20(2) (2011): 217–238.

[2] S. Dimidjian et al., "Randomized Trial of Behavioral Activation, Cognitive Therapy, and Antidepressant Medication in the Acute Treatment of Adults with Major Depression," *Journal of Consulting and Clinical Psychology* 74(4) (2006): 658–670.

[3] F. Strack, L. L. Martin, and S. Stepper, "Inhibiting and facilitating conditions of the human smile: A nonobtrusive test of the facial feedback hypothesis," *Journal of Personality and Social Psychology* 54(5) (1988): 768–777.

> *If you practice this pattern (of getting out of bed) four or five times, you will no longer find it difficult.*
> Kitzur Shulchan Aruch, Orach Chaim 1:4

This source, as well as many others in Torah literature, emphasizes the importance of routine and habits in determining behavior. Similarly, many modern self-help books and successful individuals identify ingrained daily patterns as the secret to achieving one's goals. Cognitive behavioral therapists will often help patients practice daily behaviors that are designed to improve their quality of life. The benefits of establishing good habits are also supported by research findings showing that habits help the brain conserve mental energy and thus require less willpower. Once a habit is firmly established through a series of repetitions, it can be performed in "autopilot" mode, with minimal effort and awareness. MIT neuroscientist Ann Graybiel demonstrated this effect using chocolate and rats in a maze. The first few times the rats navigated the maze in pursuit of the chocolate, their brain activity was very high. However, as they learned the path to the chocolate through repeated trials, their brain activity actually decreased significantly.[4] Anyone who has the same commute, or performs the same occupational tasks

---

4   A. B. Tort, M. A. Kramer, C. Thorn, D. J. Gibson, Y. Kubota, A. M. Graybiel, and N. J. Kopell, "Dynamic Cross-Frequency Couplings of Local Field Potential Oscillations in Rat Striatum and Hippocampus during

nearly every day, can attest to this phenomenon. The key is to apply this formula to activities that promote healthier living as well. Scheduling and following through with tasks on a consistent basis, like exercising, meditating, studying, or writing, will establish neuro-pathways in the brain. The more the routine is repeated, the deeper the pathways and the easier it becomes to follow through the next time.

3. MONITORING PROGRESS INCREASES YOUR CHANCES OF SUCCESS

והא איהו דאנן מנן להו, מיומא טבא דפסחא. ואנן מנן יומי ושבועי, והא איתערו חברייא, מצה לממני יומי, ומצוה למימני שבועי. כי בכל יומא אפיק לן מחילא דמסאבו, ואעיל לן בחילא דדכיו.

When we count the forty-nine days of the Omer from the second night of the festival, it reminds us that each day marks a step away from the defilement of Egypt and a step toward spiritual purity. At the end of this period, the Israelites were worthy of receiving the Torah.[5]

Zohar Chadash, Yisro

The mitzvah of counting the forty-nine days between Pesach and Shavuos, and specifically in an ascending order

---

Performance of a T-Maze Task," *Proceedings of the National Academy of Sciences* 105(51) (2008): 20517–20522.

5   Translation from Eliyahu Kitov, *The Book of Our Heritage*, vol. 2 (Jerusalem: Feldheim, 1992), p. 683.

with no interruptions, has been increasingly used as an important model of self-improvement by contemporary Rabbinic leaders and Jewish educators.[6] A common theme is the importance of making small, tangible improvements—coupled with a monitoring of the progress made each day, in the form of a daily count.[7] The rationale behind this self-help model is that keeping track of daily progress simultaneously maintains accountability and motivation. That is, a person is more likely to follow through with a resolution if he consistently measures steps taken toward achieving the goal. This effect has been demonstrated in research studies, which have also discovered specific strategies for self-assessment that prove to be effective. A recent meta-analysis of many psychological studies found that the more progress is monitored, the more likely we are to reach our goals. Additionally, physically recording our progress and reporting on it to others increases our chances of success even more.[8] This technique of monitoring progress is common in mental health treatment as well, especially with cognitive behavioral therapy (CBT), which typically involves recording symptom levels and measurable

---

6   See *Likutei Sichos*, vol. VII, p. 284.
7   See Akiva Tatz, *Living Inspired* (Jerusalem: Targum Press, 1993).
8   B. Harkin, T. L. Webb, B. P. Chang, A. Prestwich, M. Conner, I. Kellar,…and P. Sheeran, "Does Monitoring Goal Progress Promote Goal Attainment? A Meta-Analysis of the Experimental Evidence," *Psychological Bulletin* 142(2) (2016): 198.

gains on a frequent basis. In fact, studies have shown that therapists and patients who use formal measures of progress have improved treatment outcomes.[9]

4. HOW EMOTIONAL REASONING DISTORTS OUR THINKING

> ונהי בעינינו כחגבים: שנפל לבבנו, וזה אות לנו שלא נכבשם, כדכתיב בשאול (שמואל א' כ"ח) וירא שאול את מחנה פלשתים וירא ויחרד לבו מאד. פירוש, ע"י שנפל מורא בלבבו, חרד לבו שאות הוא כי לא יצליח.
>
> ***We were like grasshoppers in their eyes:*** *Our hearts were downcast, and this was why we believed we would be overcome. Similarly, it is written, "And Shaul saw the Philistine camp, and he was fearful and his heart trembled." Meaning that since he felt fear in his heart, it led him to believe that he would not be successful.*
>
> – Ha'amek Davar to Bamidbar 13:33

This passage describes the tendency to rely on intense (negative) emotions to inform our judgments and perceptions. Thinking thoughts and feeling emotions are two different internal processes, each of which can be helpful in making decisions. However, when we feel intensely distressed, our

---

[9] R. J. Reese, L. A. Norsworthy, and S. R. Rowlands, "Does a Continuous Feedback System Improve Psychotherapy Outcome?" *Psychotherapy: Theory, Research, Practice, Training* 46 (2009): 418–431.

emotions tend to cloud our thinking and drown out our rationality. Aaron Beck, the father of Cognitive Therapy, referred to this as "emotional reasoning" in his list of cognitive distortions.[10] Emotional reasoning involves assuming that because we feel a certain way, our associated thoughts must be true as well. For example, when someone feels anxious and afraid about taking a test, they may falsely assume that they don't know the material and will surely fail. Recent neurobiological research has helped explain how this process unfolds. It starts with an "activating event," or environmental stimulus, that triggers sudden emotional arousal. Next, the amygdala cues the release of cortisol into the bloodstream, which decreases activity in the prefrontal cortex and hippocampal brain areas. This leads to the inhibition of cognitive processes and impairs our ability to think logically.[11] However, consistent data from psychological science has shown that with proper training and enough practice, it is possible to overcome these natural biological processes and learn to override even intense emotions with rational thought.[12]

---

10 A. T. Beck and G. Emery, *Anxiety Disorders and Phobias: A Cognitive Perspective* (New York: Basic Books, 1985).
11 J. LeDoux, *The Emotional Brain* (London: Orion Books Ltd., 2003).
12 S. G. Hofmann, A. Asnaani, I. J. Vonk, A. T. Sawyer, and A. Fang, "The Efficacy of Cognitive Behavioral Therapy: A Review of Meta-Analyses," *Cognitive Therapy and Research* 36(5) (2012): 427–440.

5. POSITIVE LANGUAGE CAN HELP IMPROVE YOUR ATTITUDE

ונאמר על אחד מן החסידים, שעבר על נבלת כלב מסרחת מאד, ואמרו לו תלמידיו כמה מסרחת נבילה זאת, אמר להם כמה לבנים שיניה....והיתה כוונתו להוכיחם שלא ילמדו לשונם לדבר רע וישוב להם טבע. וכן כשילמדו לשונם לדבר טוב, ישוב להם טבע קבוע.

It is told about a pious man who passed by an extremely foul-smelling carcass of a dog. His students said to him, "How foul-smelling is this carcass!" He replied, "How white are its teeth!" His intent was to correct them, so that they not habituate to speaking negatively, as it would become their nature. For when one trains himself to use positive language, it becomes part of his natural instinct.

Duties of the Heart, "Gate of Humility," chap. 6

This passage from *Duties of the Heart* emphasizes how language impacts our perceptions of reality. The way we speak, whether internally or aloud to others, can change the nature of our experience. Modern psychology has revealed that an excellent strategy for individuals with anxiety or depression to improve their emotional states is simply by using more positive language. This is because many emotional disorders tend to be accompanied by a "negative cognitive bias," which involves a greater likelihood of interpreting events and circumstances in a manner that is negatively skewed. As such, catching negative cognitive biases in action and deliberately reframing them with positive thoughts is a scientifically proven method for changing one's mood.[13] As the excerpt above points out, human beings have the capacity to be positive even in the presence of genuinely negative stimuli (e.g., a rotting dog carcass). While realism and optimism have their relative costs and benefits from a mental health perspective,[14] the fact remains that ultimately, through frequent practice, we can choose our perspectives on life.

Credits: Rabbi Benjamin Kestenbaum, Woodmere, NY

6. MIND OVER MATTER: HOW POSITIVE THINKING CHANGES YOU

Tracht gut, vet zein gut—Think good, and it will be good.

Tzemach Tzedek, Rabbi Menachem Mendel of Lubavitch

The widespread belief that maintaining a positive attitude is the key to overcoming challenges has a basis in Torah. According to this famous Chassidic teaching, thinking

---

13 L. S. Hallion and A. M. Ruscio, "A Meta-Analysis of the Effect of Cognitive Bias Modification on Anxiety and Depression," *Psychological Bulletin* 137(6) (2011): 940.

14 L. Bortolotti and M. Antrobus, "Costs and Benefits of Realism and Optimism," *Current Opinion in Psychiatry* 28(2) (2015): 194.

positively and trusting in God's benevolence can lead to favorable outcomes through Divine providence. While psychological science has yet to explore whether positive thinking affects the universe at large, there is ample evidence that positive thinking has beneficial mental and physical health benefits. Dr. Barbara Fredrickson, a researcher from the University of North Carolina at Chapel Hill, developed the "Broaden-and-Build" theory based on her observations of experiments examining the short- and long-term effects of positive emotions. In one of her studies, when participants were randomly assigned to watch films that induced positive emotions (e.g., amusement), they were better at creative and "big-picture" thinking than those who watched films that induced negative (e.g., fear or sadness) or no explicit emotions.[15] Long-term benefits such as resilience and resourcefulness are also associated with positive attitudes. In a study exploring the traumatic effects of the 9/11 attacks, Fredrickson found that positive emotions such as gratitude and love served as protective factors against depression.[16] She explained that

---

15   B. L. Fredrickson, "The Value of Positive Emotions," *American Scientist* 91 (2003): 330–335.

16   B. L. Fredrickson, M. M. Tugade, C. E. Waugh, and G. R. Larkin, "What Good Are Positive Emotions in Crisis? A prospective study of resilience and emotions following the terrorist attacks on the United States on September 11th, 2001," *Journal of Personality and Social Psychology* 84(2) (2003): 365.

positive feelings are not merely temporary distractions but are actually the key ingredient for coping and thriving during adversity. Thus, one way that positive thinking can impact us (and the world) is via cognitive broadening. While fear and panic create autonomic arousal and therefore action-oriented responses (i.e., fight or flight), positive emotions induce greater cognitive functioning, expansiveness, long-term planning, perspective taking, and other adaptive ways of thinking.

7. COGNITIVE REFRAMING HELPS US OVERCOME ADVERSITY

> וְעַתָּה אַל תֵּעָצְבוּ וְאַל יִחַר בְּעֵינֵיכֶם כִּי מְכַרְתֶּם אֹתִי הֵנָּה כִּי לְמִחְיָה שְׁלָחַנִי אֱלֹהִים לִפְנֵיכֶם:
>
> *Do not be sad, and don't let it trouble you that you sold me here. I was sent by God before you to sustain our lives.*
>
> Bereishis 45:5

Yosef's ability to reflect on all the trials and tribulations he experienced in his life and see the purpose of it all is truly remarkable. He was sold as a slave by his brothers, thrown in jail for a crime he never committed, and waited twenty-two years to see his dreams fulfilled—without ever hearing words of encouragement from God. At the end of it all, he tells his brothers basically, "Don't you see? It was all meant to be!" He urges them not to bear the guilt of what happened to him, for it was all part of God's plan.

This inspiring passage demonstrates how Yosef applied an essential element of Cognitive Therapy called "cognitive reframing." Cognitive reframing is predicated on the idea that our interpretations of events influence our emotions.[17] Cognitive therapy teaches that maintaining cognitive distortions, which are negatively biased or irrational interpretations of our experience, leads to negative feelings, such as depression, guilt, pessimism, anger, and worry. One example of a cognitive distortion is "personalization," which refers to the tendency for a person to believe that they are personally responsible for causing negative events.[18] In this regard, cognitive reframing is a psychotherapy technique in which a therapist helps others to reinterpret past events from a more positive and rational perspective. In the above verse, Yosef was helping his brothers reframe their experience in a positive light and see that God imbued his predicament with meaning. Notably, psychological research has found that religious beliefs can play a strong role in

---

17 A. Ellis, "The Revised ABC's of Rational-Emotive Therapy (RET)," *Journal of Rational-Emotive and Cognitive-Behavior Therapy* 9(3) (1991): 139–172; A. T. Beck, "The Past and Future of Cognitive Therapy," *The Journal of Psychotherapy Practice and Research* 6(4) (1997): 276; M. E. P. Seligman, *Authentic Happiness* (New York: Free Press, 2002).

18 M. E. P. Seligman, *Learned Optimism* (New York: Free Press, 2008).

shaping people's perspectives and emotions. In one study among physically ill individuals, people who viewed their illnesses as a form of punishment from God had not only lower quality of life but poorer physical health and even lower cognitive functioning.[19] However, people who interpreted their illness as a benevolent act of God tended to have better overall health.

Credits: Rabbi Lord Jonathan Sacks, former Chief Rabbi of the UK

8. COGNITIVE DISTORTIONS LEAD TO POOR CHOICES

ומן החזק שבשלוחיו אשר יורה ולחם אותך בהם במצפון ענינך שישתדל לספק עליך אמתתך ולשבש מה שנתברר לך ולערבב את נפשך במחשבות כזבים וטענות שקרים יטריד אותך בהם מתעולותיך ויספק עליך מה שנתברר לך מאמונתך ודעתך.

Among the strongest of his weapons in the evil inclination's arsenal that he will fire at you and wage war in your innermost being is to try to cast doubt in your mind about true notions, confound what is clear to you, confuse your mind with inaccurate thoughts and erroneous arguments, draw you away from what is for

---

19 K. I. Pargament, H. G. Koenig, N. Tarakeshwar, and J. Hahn, "Religious Coping Methods as Predictors of Psychological, Physical and Spiritual Outcomes among Medically Ill Elderly Patients: A Two-Year Longitudinal Study," *Journal of Health Psychology* 9(6), (2004): 713–730.

your benefit, and cause you to doubt what is clear to you in your doctrines and beliefs.

Duties of the Heart, "Gate of Devoted Action," chap. 5

This passage describes how the evil inclination uses deceptive yet convincing arguments to imbue a sense of doubt, create confusion, impair judgment, and lead us to negative conclusions. This description is similar to how cognitive therapists, such as Aaron Beck and David Burns, teach the concept of cognitive distortions. Although we may like to believe that we are always rational, objective observers of our environment, the truth is that our perceptions easily become biased and inaccurate. Beck developed a list of over a dozen "thinking-traps" he called cognitive distortions. For instance, "over-generalization" refers to generating a pattern or conclusion from one event or data point. "Mental filter" is when we become overly sensitive to negative stimuli (e.g., failure, rejection) and fail to even perceive neutral or positive events (e.g., successes, competence). Like the evil inclination, these distortions could easily influence our actions, such as when someone with social anxiety avoids going to a party because of an embarrassing memory from a previous social engagement.

9. ACTION BEGETS LEARNING: THE IMPORTANCE OF BEHAVIOR CHANGE IN PSYCHOTHERAPY

וַיֹּאמְרוּ כֹּל אֲשֶׁר דִּבֶּר ה' נַעֲשֶׂה וְנִשְׁמָע...ברישא עשי והדר לשמוע.

"Everything that God commanded us we will do and we will understand." First, they acted and then they understood.

Talmud Bavli, *Shabbos* 88a

The second interpretation—not the plain sense of the text but important nonetheless—has been given often in modern Jewish thought. On this view na'aseh v'nishma means, "We will do and we will understand." From this they derive the conclusion that we can only understand Judaism by doing it, by performing the commands and living a Jewish life. In the beginning is the deed; only afterward comes the grasp, the insight, the comprehension.

Rabbi Lord Jonathan Sacks,
Covenant and Conversation: Mishpatim, 5776

This central concept of Judaism prioritizes action over knowledge.

A modern psychological interpretation is that behavioral engagement is a necessary precursor to comprehension of abstract material. When teaching someone a skill, it is more effective to instruct them in praxis, having them rehearse and practice the new behavior, rather than just telling them what to do. This is utilized in modern therapeutic treatments, which often incorporate role-play in order to bolster skills-building. For instance, in one highly effective form of CBT for children with disruptive behavior disorders called Parent Child Interaction Therapy (PCIT), the therapist tells parents about effective language and parenting behaviors immediately before asking the parents to engage with their children during the session.[20] The entire process of acquiring and mastering the new parenting skills is done with repetitive action via live coaching sessions: the therapist observes the parents interacting with their children from behind a one-way mirror, and provides feedback to them via a Bluetooth headset. Although it is important for the parents to understand the rationale of why the new skills are more effective, there is little emphasis and relatively minimal time dedicated to the theoretical underpinnings, and the majority of sessions are spent making behavior changes *in vivo*. This is because research has shown that there is little benefit in teaching the skills alone with no practice, as it is unlikely in that case that parents will demonstrate significant changes in their parenting behaviors.[21]

---

20 S. Eyberg and P. Durning, *Parent-Child Interaction Therapy: Procedures Manual* (University of Chicago, School of Social Service Administration, 1994).

21 P. A. Knapp and R. H. Deluty, "Relative Effectiveness of Two Behavioral Parent Training Programs," *Journal of Clinical Child Psychology* 18 (1989): 314–322.

10. TEFILLIN AND COGNITIVE DISSONANCE: SYNCHRONIZING BELIEFS AND BEHAVIORS

Through this powerful mitzvah, engaging both the arm (our actions) and the eye (our outlook and thoughts), we continue the Divine process that God initiated in Egypt with a "strong arm."

Rabbi Avraham Yitzchak Hakohen Kook,
Gold from the Land of Israel, Parashas Bo

Many Torah scholars have offered interpretations for the deeper meaning of the mitzvah of tefillin. A common theme is the unification of action (represented by tefillin *shel yad*—arm) and mind (represented by tefillin *shel rosh*—head). This is stressed even in the practical guidelines of donning and removing tefillin, in that one should not interrupt the process either mentally or verbally between the two actions. Similarly, one should not ever wear only the tefillin on the head without having it on the arm. This emphasis on synchronizing one's actions with one's beliefs is reminiscent of the well-known psychological principle of cognitive dissonance. Developed by Leon Festinger, the theory of cognitive dissonance posits that when we engage in behaviors that contradict our deepest beliefs, we experience psychological discomfort.[22] In order to

---

22 L. Festinger, *A Theory of Cognitive Dissonance* (California: Stanford University Press, 1957).

resolve this conflict, we seek to change either our actions or our beliefs to restore harmony. Although it is more reasonable to modify our behaviors to be more in line with our beliefs, in actuality it is far more difficult to change behavior and much simpler to justify or adjust our attitudes.[23] For instance, someone addicted to cigarettes may experience cognitive dissonance since they know smoking is extremely harmful to their health yet they do it anyway. Instead of quitting smoking, it takes much less energy to rationalize their behavior by telling themselves "it won't happen to me."[24] The message of tefillin is that one cannot wear the *shel rosh*—maintaining belief, unless he is wearing the *shel yad*—exhibiting the behavior, as well.

11. TESHUVAH GEMURAH AND RELAPSE PREVENTION: PRACTICE MAKES PERFECT

אי זו היא תשובה גמורה? זה שבא לידו דבר שעבר בו ואפשר בידו לעשותו ופרש ולא עשה מפני התשובה. לא מיראה ולא מכשלון כח.

What is complete repentance? He who is presented with an opportunity to repeat a sin from his past and refrained from doing so because of his commitment

---

23 Ibid.
24 O. Fotuhi, G. T. Fong, M. P. Zanna, R. Borland, H. H. Yong, and K. M. Cummings, "Patterns of Cognitive Dissonance-Reducing Beliefs among Smokers: A Longitudinal Analysis from the International Tobacco Control (ITC) Four Country Survey," *Tobacco Control* 22(1) (2013): 52–58.

to change, not out of fear of consequences or a lack of ability to sin.

Rambam, Hilchos Teshuvah 2:1

The *Rambam* elaborates on the various stages and processes of *teshuvah* later in that chapter, but in this famous excerpt, he describes the highest level of repentance: facing the same situation as one was in when they previously sinned and overcoming one's negative internal tendencies. As a great scholar and physician, the *Rambam's* approach remains effective even today as a method used by some clinical scientists who study relapse prevention for addiction to alcohol and/or chemical substances. Notably, one-year relapse rates for alcohol and tobacco cessation programs are astronomically high (80–95%).[25] Therefore, clinical science strongly encourages *all* individuals who struggle with addiction to refrain from *any* experience, emotion, setting, thought, or context that presents an increased risk for a person to engage in some transgressive behavior.[26] Similarly, *all* who struggle with addiction are encouraged to maintain adequate self-care and social support, and to learn and practice coping skills such

---

25 C. S. Hendershot, K. Witkiewitz, W. H. George, and G. A. Marlatt, "Relapse Prevention for Addictive Behaviors," *Substance Abuse Treatment, Prevention, and Policy* 6(1) (2011): 17.

26 K. A. Witkiewitz and G. A. Marlatt (eds.), *Therapist's Guide to Evidence-Based Relapse Prevention* (Academic Press, 2011), p. 5.

as mindfulness in order to cope with day-to-day cravings. However, in order to make treatment ultimately effective, some clinical scientists maintain that some addicts can benefit from cue exposure, which involves confronting tempting circumstances and resisting the urge to engage in addictive behavior. Typically, cue exposure therapy is practiced in a controlled laboratory setting and not in the real world, in order to minimize potential risk for relapse. However, the point remains that practicing acts of self-control *in vivo* is a key factor to overcoming one's tendencies to indulge.[27]

---

[27] M. Muraven, "Practicing Self-Control Lowers the Risk of Smoking Lapse," *Psychology of Addictive Behaviors* 24(3) (2010): 446.

Chapter 2

DIALECTICAL

BEHAVIOR

THERAPY

1. OPPOSITE ACTION CAN CHANGE YOUR EMOTIONS

מי שהוא בעל חמה אומרים לו להנהיג עצמו שאם הכה וקלל לא ירגיש כלל. וילך בדרך זו זמן מרבה עד שיתעקר החמה מלבו. ואם היה גבה לב ינהיג עצמו בביזיון הרבה וישב למטה מן הכל וילבש בלויי סחבות המב־ זות את לובשיהם וכיוצא בדברים אלו עד שיעקר גבה הלב ממנו...ועל קו זה יעשה בשאר כל הדעות אם היה רחוק לקצה האחד ירחיק עצמו לקצה השני וינהג בו זמן רב עד שיחזור בו לדרך הטובה.

One who gets angry should be taught that if he is injured or cursed, he should let go of his negativity over and over until his anger is uprooted from his heart. One who is arrogant should accustom himself to self-abasement by assuming an uncoveted position, wearing rags and other shameful clothing, and similar things, until his haughtiness is uprooted...In this manner, regarding all character traits, one who is unbalanced in one direction should distance himself to the opposite extreme for a protracted period of time, until he can return to a good, balanced way of life.

Rambam, Mishneh Torah, Hilchos De'os 2:2

Here, the *Rambam* describes a similar concept to the one above, but takes it a step further: by acting in an *opposite manner* to how we feel, we can change our character traits (and emotions). This concept is widely used today in Dialectical Behavior Therapy (DBT) and is known as "opposite action," which involves changing emotions by action opposite to the present way in which one feels. Common examples of opposite action in DBT include choosing to be social when you feel like withdrawing from others, taking on a challenging project when you feel afraid to fail, getting moving when you feel lethargic, approaching others to connect when you fear that you will be rejected, and being kind to others when you feel irritated and annoyed. This approach has been substantiated as an effective and key strategy in treating an array of clinical problems today, including depression, anxiety, and as the *Rambam* suggests, anger and haughtiness (narcissism).[1]

---

1   S. L. Rizvi and M. M. Linehan, "The Treatment of Maladaptive Shame in Borderline Personality Disorder: A Pilot Study of 'Opposite Action,'" *Cognitive and Behavioral Practice* 12(4) (2005): 437–447.

2. VALIDATING THE EMOTIONAL PAIN OF SELF-INJURY

וְשֶׂרֶט לָנֶפֶשׁ לֹא תִתְּנוּ בִּבְשַׂרְכֶם וּכְתֹבֶת קַעֲקַע לֹא תִתְּנוּ בָּכֶם אֲנִי ה'.

You shall not make cuts in your flesh for the dead, nor etch any tattoos on yourselves: I am Hashem.

Vayikra 19:28

בָּנִים אַתֶּם לַה' אֱלֹקֵיכֶם, לֹא תִתְגֹּדְדוּ וְלֹא תָשִׂימוּ קָרְחָה בֵּין עֵינֵיכֶם לָמֵת.

You are children of Hashem, your God. [Therefore,] do not cut yourself and do not create bald spots at the top of your head, when mourning the dead.

Devarim 14:1

וטעם **בנים**. אחר שתדעו שאתם בנים לשם והוא אוהב אתכם יותר מהאב לבן אל תתגודדו על כל מה שיעשה כי כל אשר יעשה לטוב הוא ואם לא תבינוהו כאשר לא יבינו הבנים הקטנים מעשה אביהם רק יסמכו עליו כן תעשו גם אתם כי עם קדוש אתה ואינך כשאר כל הגוים על כן לא תעשה כמעשיהם.

The reason why the verse says "children" is so that you should know that you are the children of Hashem, and He loves you more than a father loves a son. Therefore, do not cut yourselves even when [bad] things happen, for everything He does is for the good. Even if you can't understand it at the time, be like the child who doesn't understand his parent's actions, but simply trusts and relies on them. For you are a holy nation, not like the other nations who act this way.

Commentary of the *Ibn Ezra*

Unfortunately, it is common today for individuals with emotional instability, especially adolescents, to engage in self-injury. Although peers and family members are deeply alarmed by the behavior, often perceiving it as analogous to—or even preparation for—suicide, self-injurious behaviors typically represent a misplaced form of self-treatment. Individuals often harm themselves to cope with extreme emotional pain when they lack more positive coping methods. Many self-injurers report temporary relief from emotional pain when they perform acts of self-harm, as well as a false sense of control and distraction.[2] The problem is that self-injury is no panacea; negative emotions always return, and in fact, they usually worsen. Therefore, one of the main goals of DBT treatment is to teach self-injurers more effective skills to manage strong negative emotions. It's important to recognize that self-injury is not simply "crazy," and it is neither an indulgent attention-seeking scheme nor a sign of giving up. In the above verse, it is noteworthy that Torah recognizes some people's tendency to self-injure when they

---

2   M. K. Nock, "Why Do People Hurt Themselves? New Insights into the Nature and Functions of Self-Injury," *Current Directions in Psychological Science* 18(2) (2009): 78–83.

are very distressed and prohibits the practice, which modern psychology has identified as an unsustainable and maladaptive coping strategy. Note as well that the verse ends with the words "I am Hashem," as if to say that God Himself is validating the urge to self-injure, but nevertheless urges the Jewish People not to engage in this behavior.

3. WISE MIND: THE HARMONIOUS BALANCE OF EMOTION AND INTELLECT

> *Man cannot live with intellect alone, nor with emotion alone. Intellect and emotion must forever be joined together…[otherwise] he will lose his ability to feel, and his flaws and deficiencies will be myriad despite the strength of his intellect…If he sinks into unmitigated emotion, he will fall to the depths of foolishness…Only the quality of equilibrium, which balances intellect with emotion, can deliver him completely.*
>
> Rabbi Avraham Yitzchak Hakohen Kook[3]

In this passage, Rav Kook beautifully describes "wise mind," which is a popular concept in the practice of DBT. The concept of wise mind holds that emotional wellness occurs only when one achieves balance between one's emotions and

---

3   B. Ish-Shalom, *Rav Avraham Itzhak HaCohen Kook: Between Rationalism and Mysticism* (SUNY Press, 2012), p. 152.

one's intellect.[4] DBT refers to the intellect as "reasonable mind" and emotions as "emotional mind." When we operate with our reasonable mind, we tend to be logical, rational, and calculated. Conversely, when we are intensely passionate, impulsive, or sensitive, our emotional mind is in charge. As DBT explains—and Rav Kook as well—functioning solely in either of these two states is unhealthy, and the ultimate goal is to get to a place of wise mind, in which one integrates both intellect and emotions to achieve true wisdom. In psychologist Marshal Linehan's words, a wise mind is the synthesis of "direct experience, immediate cognition, and the grasping of the meaning, significance, or truth of an event."[5] Simply put, the objective is to recognize and respect our emotions while responding in a rational manner.

4. MINDFULNESS AND THE MENORAH: THE CALMING CANDLE MEDITATION

הנרות הללו קדש הם ואין לנו רשות להשתמש בהם, אלא לראותם בלבד ...

---

[4] M. M. Linehan, *Skills Training Manual for Treating Borderline Personality Disorder* (New York: Guilford Publications, 1993).

[5] M. M. Linehan, *Cognitive-Behavioral Treatment of Borderline Personality Disorder* (New York: The Guilford Press, 1993), p. 214.

Dialectical Behavior Therapy

These Chanukah candles are holy, and we are not to make any practical use of them, but just gaze upon them.

Haneros Hallalu, birchos Chanukah

מאן דבעי למנדע חכמתא דיחודא קדישא, יסתכל בשלהובא דסלקא מגו גחלתא, או מגו בוצינא דדליק.

One who seeks to contemplate the Divine wisdom should meditate on a flame rising from a coal or candle.

Zohar 1:50b

While many objects involved in mitzvos serve some practical purpose (e.g., Shabbos candles are meant to provide light), the Chanukah candles are unique in that we are prohibited from deriving any utilitarian benefit from them. Rather, we are only to gaze upon their light, which the *Zohar*, in another context, prescribes as a holy meditation exercise. The *Zohar* explains further that by focusing on the various colors of a flame and meditating on their spiritual attributes, one can achieve enlightenment. This sacred candle meditation is reminiscent of mindfulness exercises, which are commonly integrated into modern therapeutic practice and involve concerted focus on specific sensory stimuli with the aim of quelling anxiety and maladaptive thought patterns.[6] The es-

---

6 J. Gu, C. Strauss, R. Bond, and K. Cavanagh, "How do mindfulness-based cognitive therapy and mindfulness-based stress reduction improve

sence of mindfulness is "paying attention in a particular way: on purpose, in the present moment, and nonjudgmentally."[7] By focusing on a particular sense—sight, sound, smell, taste or touch—we are able to calm our minds and live fully in the present. Interestingly, it is not uncommon in some forms of modern psychotherapy (e.g., DBT) to use a candle as a focus for mindfulness mediation: patients are encouraged to sit in a dark room and mindfully watch the candle flame flicker.[8] This technique has been known to improve concentration and mood, and to decrease anxiety.[9] It also can help with feeling connected to spiritual wisdom, as the passage above from the *Zohar* suggests.

5. USING DIALECTICAL THINKING TO BALANCE CONTRADICTORY EMOTIONS

נחלקו בית שמאי ובית הלל הללו אומרים הלכה כמותנו והללו אומרים הלכה כמותנו יצאה בת קול ואמרה אלו ואלו דברי אלקים חיים הן.

---

mental health and well-being? A systematic review and meta-analysis of mediation studies." *Clinical Psychology Review* 37 (2015): 1–12.

7   J. Kabat-Zinn, *Wherever You Go, There You Are: Mindfulness Meditation in Everyday Life* (New York: Hyperion, 1994), p. 4.

8   A. Rosen, *Lasting Transformation: A Guide to Navigating Life's Journey* (Balboa Press, 2010).

9   D. M. Davis and J. A. Hayes, "What Are the Benefits of Mindfulness? A Practice Review of Psychotherapy-Related Research," *Psychotherapy* 48(2) (2011):198.

There was an ongoing debate between the Academy of Hillel and the Academy of Shammai. Each side argued their points, until finally a Heavenly voice proclaimed, "Both of these perspectives are true words of the living God!"

Talmud Bavli, Eruvin 13b

This is a well-known source for the fundamental principle of Judaism of the plurality of perspectives and the allowance for contradictory rulings. Disagreements are common and should not preclude a healthy dialogue. Like the Talmudic approach above, dialectical thinking, a foundation of DBT, teaches that the ability to simultaneously acknowledge opposing viewpoints is a key component in the process of changing oneself. DBT takes this one step further and emphasizes that all of our emotions—even when they conflict—should be validated and acknowledged. In the realm of emotions, human beings are complicated, and it is important for us to learn to live with ambiguity and multiple perspectives and feelings inside of us. Many significant experiences elicit emotional dissonance—the experience of contradictory emotions at the same time—which can seem confusing at best and distressing at worst. A common (maladaptive) coping strategy to reduce the emotional dissonance is to overemphasize one extreme and dismiss or repress the unwanted feelings. This reaction is often practiced by children.

For instance, when a child feels angry at their parent for chastising their misbehavior, it can be difficult for them to simultaneously acknowledge and cope with their feelings of shame and guilt for doing something wrong. Similarly, when adults experience complicated bereavement, such as the death of an abusive parent, they may also have contradictory negative and positive feelings. The ability to simply experience a full range of complex emotions (e.g., "I feel angry at my parent for what they did and also feel a sense of loss with their death") lends itself to healthier psychological functioning.[10]

6. SITTING WITH WILLING AND OPEN HANDS CREATES ACCEPTANCE

> כשאומרים פסוק "פותח" הנזכר, פורשים כפיהם לעיני השמים, והוא מנהג יפה לעשות בזה פועל דמיוני לקבלת מזלם את השפע מלמעלה.
>
> *While reciting the verse, "Open up your hands and provide sustenance to all life" (Tehillim 144:16), it is a good practice to actually perform this action and sit with your palms open toward the sky, in order to accept the Heavenly assistance.*
>
> Rabbi Yosef Chaim of Baghdad,
> *Ben Ish Chai, Parashas Vayigash* 1:12

---

10   M. M. Linehan, *Cognitive-Behavioral Treatment of Borderline Personality Disorder* (New York: The Guilford Press, 1993).

It is a widespread custom among Sephardic Jews to practice this ritual of placing one's hands forward on the lap, with the palms open and facing skyward during this prayer. This is both a symbolic and metaphysical gesture of accepting God's grace and receiving blessings.[11] It is also quite similar to the acceptance skill of "willing hands"—which is commonly used today in DBT. "Willing hands" involves performing the same actions described above and is meant to help synchronize the body and mind. When someone is stressed or angry, their body tenses up and they tend to clench their fists. By contrast, "willing hands" helps a person to accept reality and become one with unpleasant results. By engaging in a willing body posture, we can adopt a more accepting attitude. As the DBT manual states, "Remember, your hands communicate to your brain; your body connects to your mind."[12] Individuals are encouraged to practice this technique when they are struggling to find peace.

---

11   See Rabbi Eliezer Yehuda Waldenberg, *Tzitz Eliezer* 12:8.
12   M. M. Linehan, "Distress Tolerance Handout 14," *DBT Skills Training Handouts and Worksheets*, second edition.

7. MAKING TIME FOR MINDFULNESS TO FIND PEACE OF MIND

> אך מפסידי החסידות הם הטרדות והדאגות, כי בהיות השכל טרוד ונחפז בדאגותיו ובעסקיו, אי אפשר לו לפנות אל ההתבוננות הזה, ומבלי התבוננות לא ישיג החסידות.
>
> *The barriers to piety are distractions and worries. For when the mind is preoccupied and distressed with anxieties and daily affairs, it is impossible to find mental space for reflection, and reflection is the prerequisite for spiritual growth.*
>
> Rabbi Moshe Chaim Luzzatto,
> *Mesillas Yesharim*, chap. 21

Here, in the *Ramchal*'s famous guidebook for spiritual growth, he warns of the detriments of mental preoccupation. He preaches the importance of having "down-time" and mental respite from daily worries, for it is in moments of introspection that we can reflect on our lives. Modern culture, especially in fast-paced urban areas, tends to overvalue productivity and efficiency, leading to hasty activity, tight schedules, and little time to reflect. One's ability to multitask has become a badge of honor, and technology has exacerbated our constant preoccupation. However, an abundance of psychological research has found that multitasking is actually ineffective and can have long-term negative consequences on our stress levels, attention span, and health.[13] Therefore, mindfulness—the act of focusing our attention on the present—allows for a fuller, richer experience of our environment. Mindfulness is one of the core components of DBT, and DBT skills groups integrate mindfulness practices in each session. In recent years, this approach has gained tremendous popularity in both psychotherapy and mainstream culture, with very promising research results.[14]

8. PATIENCE IS THE ABILITY TO TOLERATE SUFFERING

וְהוֹצֵאתִי אֶתְכֶם מִתַּחַת **סִבְלֹת** מִצְרָיִם.

I [Hashem] will free you from the burdens of Egypt.

Shemos 6:6

ומהי סבלנות? הסבלן דומה ממש לאדם הנושא משא כבד, ואף שהוא כבד עליו הוא ממשיך ללכת בדרכו ואינו נלאה לשאתו.

---

13 http://www.apa.org/research/action/multitask.aspx; E. Ophir, C. Nass, and A. D. Wagner, "Cognitive Control in Media Multitaskers," *Proceedings of the National Academy of Sciences* 106(37) (2009): 15583–15587.

14 N. Raja-Khan, K. Agito, J. Shah, C. M. Stetter, T. S. Gustafson, H. Socolow,…and R. S. Legro, "Mindfulness-Based Stress Reduction in Women with Overweight or Obesity: A Randomized Clinical Trial," *Obesity* 25(8) (2017): 1349–1359. Also, M. Xu, C. Purdon, P. Seli, and D. Smilek, "Mindfulness and Mind Wandering: The Protective Effects of Brief Meditation in Anxious Individuals," *Consciousness and Cognition* 51 (2017): 157–165.

What is patience? The patient person is like someone who is carrying a heavy load, and even though it weighs on him, he continues on his way and does not tire of carrying it.

Rav Shlomo Wolbe, *Alei Shur*, vol. 2, 7:1

Rav Wolbe explains that the character trait of patience ultimately stems from one's ability to tolerate discomfort, suffering, and distress. This is learned from the fact that the Hebrew word for "burdens," סבלות (from the *pasuk* above), shares the same etymological root as the word for "patience," סבלנות.[15] Therefore, a person's level of impatience is not due to impetuousness or impulsivity, but rather the extent to which they can accept distress by tolerating and holding the pain of negative feelings without allowing their emotions to take over their behaviors. Interestingly, most modern anger management techniques do not take this approach; rather, angry individuals are typically taught to remain calm, count to ten, and simply wait for their anger to subside. Perhaps for this reason, modern anger management approaches are notoriously ineffective, and their effects are more a function of pre-treatment levels of anger than engagement in a program.[16]

---

15 See Rabbi Shlomo Hakohen Rabinowicz, *Tiferes Shlomo, Parashas Va'era*.
16 K. Howells, A. Day, P. Williamson, et al., "Brief Anger Management Programs with Offenders: Outcomes and Predictors of Change," *The Journal of Forensic Psychiatry and Psychology* 16(2) (2005): 296–311.

Rav Wolbe would seem to suggest that the core component of anger management is acceptance—for an individual to bear the burden of suffering and accept a lack of control over others' behaviors and idiosyncrasies. This concept has been broadly utilized in DBT. In fact, in the DBT module related to "distress tolerance," patients are taught to "carry the load" of temporary emotional pain through radically accepting distress without engaging in harmful behaviors.

Credits: Rabbi Leib Kelemen

Chapter 3

GENERAL

PSYCHOTHERAPY

1. UNCONDITIONAL POSITIVE REGARD

ה' ה', אני הוא קודם שיחטא האדם ואני הוא לאחר שיחטא האדם ויעשה תשובה.

"Hashem, Hashem…" should be understood as follows: I am He before a person sins, and I am He after a person sins and repents.

Talmud Bavli, Rosh Hashanah 17b

The Talmud teaches us that this verse's seemingly superfluous repetition of the Divine Name (representing God's mercy) implies that God maintains a loving, compassionate relationship with us, regardless of our misdeeds. There may be consequences for our actions, but God's love for us never ceases and our relationship is never beyond repair. Whereas in human relationships it is often difficult for it to remain intact after one party severely errs (e.g., an unfaithful partner), God's perception of us will not be damaged because of our misdeeds. This is similar to the psychotherapy concept known as Unconditional Positive Regard. Coined by the great humanistic psychologist Carl Rogers, this concept emphasizes that a therapist should always maintain an accepting and validating attitude toward patients, even if their beliefs or actions are dysfunctional or morally reprehensible.[1] According to Rogers, this is the most essential component to facilitating behavioral change, because when a person feels loved and cared for without limits, they are more likely to accept responsibility for their actions and use their internal resources to grow. Indeed, one recent psychotherapy research study confirmed that therapists' positive regard for patients is a key factor in improving treatment outcomes.[2]

2. THE TALKING CURE: HOW PSYCHOTHERAPY CAN HELP

דְּאָגָה בְלֶב אִישׁ יַשְׁחֶנָּה וְדָבָר טוֹב יְשַׂמְּחֶנָּה.

If there is worry in a man's heart, he should subdue it, and let a good word turn it to joy.

Mishlei 12:25

---

[1] Carl R. Rogers, "Client-Centered Approach to Therapy," in I. L. Kutash and A. Wolf, *Psychotherapist's Casebook* (Jossey-Bass Inc Pub, 1986).

[2] B. A. Farber and E. M. Doolin, "Positive Regard," *Psychotherapy* 48(1) (2011): 58–64.

דְּאָגָה בְלֶב אִישׁ יַשְׁחֶנָּה: רבי אמי ורבי אסי, חד אמר ישחנה מדעתו וחד אמר ישיחנה לאחרים.

Rabbi Ami and Rabbi Asi debate the meaning of this verse. One says that it means you should push it out of your mind, and the other says you should speak of it to others.

Talmud Bavli, Yoma 75a

Although the Rabbinic commentaries on this Gemara explain that the benefit of discussing one's worries with others is that they may have some practical advice or helpful words for the worrier, it could also mean that simply verbalizing it out loud to someone else can assuage the nervous feelings.

Joseph Breuer, a mentor of Sigmund Freud, coined the term "The Talking Cure" to describe how psychotherapy can help individuals with emotional distress. While talk therapy has come a long way since the days of Freud, almost all forms of psychotherapy continue to involve translating feelings into words. Patients are encouraged to verbalize their inner experiences, which tends to neutralize distress. Since negative emotions and thoughts are unpleasant, people are averse to expressing them, and most patients find it difficult to do so at first. Over time, though, simply speaking about one's worries bolsters our ability to tolerate and cope with adversity. One fascinating study demonstrated this effect with arachnophobia patients (people who have a clinical fear of spiders).[3] Participants exposed to live spiders were randomly assigned to one of four groups: (1) speaking about nothing while in the presence of the spider (exposure alone), (2) speaking about something unrelated to the spider (distraction), (3) speaking something positive about spiders (reappraisal), or (4) describing their fears (affect labeling). Those who described their fears displayed the greatest reduction of anxiety over the study, suggesting that speaking about one's worries can help alleviate them.

3. THE INFLUENCE OF SUBCONSCIOUS FORCES

One must realize that man's internal and external powers are distinct from one another. A given person may have very good external forces, while his internal ones may be very evil; while at times, the opposite may be the case.

Kisvei Rav Yisrael Salanter, 173

הוא אשר נקרא אצל חוקרי כחות נפשות האדם, כחות מאירים ברורים
או כהים [קלארע און דונקעלע], כן גם בכחות התפעלות הנפשי, ישנם
כחות מאירים [קלארע] וכהים [דונקעלע], הכהים המה יותר חזקים
ומוציאים פעלתם בהתעוררות מעט בחזק יד, אהבת האדם לצאצאיו

---

3   K. Kircanski, M. D. Lieberman, and M. G. Craske, "Feelings into Words: Contributions of Language to Exposure Therapy," *Psychological Science* 23(10) (2012): 1086–1091.

> כהים המה, וכמעט ברב העתים אינם נרגשים להאדם עצמו, ובהתעו־
> ררות קטנה תתלהב לאש בוערת, תאות האדם המה הכהים אשר בלי
> התעוררות מה, כמעט אינם נרגשים, ולזאת גדול כחם למשל באדם:

> *Those who study the inner workings of the human psyche refer to two inner forces: the light forces, "klore" (conscious), and the dark forces, "dunkle" (subconscious)[4]...[T]he dark forces are stronger, are easily awakened, and can have a strong influence on our behavior. A person's love for his/her children is a subconscious force, and isn't consciously felt on a regular basis, but it can become ignited from even the slightest trigger. One's inner desires are also subconscious forces, and are almost undetectable, yet that is why they are very powerful in driving a person's actions.*
>
> Rabbi Yisrael Salanter, *Ohr Yisrael*, chap. 6

This passage, which Rav Yisrael wrote sixty years before Sigmund Freud's *Interpretation of Dreams*, introduces the concept of the subconscious—the patterns of thought and emotion that occur outside of our conscious awareness, but nevertheless impact behavior. Just as Rav Yisrael states, it is well-known today that the subconscious plays a strong role

---

4   See "Rabbi Israel Salanter and His Psychology of Mussar Culture and Context" by Immanuel Etkes, in Arthur Green, ed., *Jewish Spirituality* (New York: Crossroad, 1989), chap. 7.

in day-to-day life. Numerous studies from psychological science have revealed that being exposed to stimuli beneath the threshold of conscious awareness can impact our judgments, impressions, and reactions. For example, presenting words on a screen for a fraction of second—so quickly that the conscious mind cannot even process having seen them—can automatically trigger responses to other words.[5] Even more profound, research has also found that many participants who consciously report non-biased views demonstrate strongly biased associations when pairing different words or stimuli with each other. Many people who say that they are not biased about gender or race will respond slower and make more cognitive errors when images of females are paired with words connoting power, and respond faster with fewer errors when pictures of African-Americans are paired with threat-related words.[6]

As Rav Yisrael suggests, change cannot happen unless one's unconscious processes are brought into cognitive awareness, and to this end, virtually all forms of modern

---

5   M. R. Klinger, P. C. Burton, and G. S. Pitts, "Mechanisms of Unconscious Priming: I. Response Competition, Not Spreading Activation," *Journal of Experimental Psychology: Learning, Memory, and Cognition* 26(2) (2000): 441.

6   A. G. Greenwald, M. R. Banaji, L. A. Rudman, S. D. Farnham, B. A. Nosek, D. S. Mellott, "A Unified Theory of Implicit Attitudes, Stereotypes, Self-Esteem, and Self-Concept," *Psychological Review* 109 (2002): 3–25.

psychotherapy involve introspection or monitoring to increase self-awareness.

Credits: Rabbi Yisroel Gelber, Baltimore, MD

4. PROJECTING OUR FLAWS ONTO OTHERS

כל הפוסל, פסול.

Anyone who disqualifies others, it is a sign that he himself is flawed.

Talmud Bavli, Kiddushin 70a

כל הנגעים אדם רואה, חוץ מנגעי עצמו.

One can notice all blemishes except for one's own.

Mishnah, Negaim 2:5

Sigmund Freud wrote about "projection," which is a subconscious process in which the psyche denies possessing a positive or negative trait in itself by seeking out the trait in someone else.[7] Freud postulated that this happens as a result of psychological immaturity, such that the individual lacks the coping capacity to accept their flaws or even their qualities, and in order to relieve feelings of guilt or anxiety they

---

7   A. Freud, *The Ego and the Mechanisms of Defence* (London: Hogarth Press, 1936).

transmit the trait onto others.[8] While psychological science has not yet fully explored this phenomenon, there seem to be many examples of projection in everyday life. For instance, many aggression-prone individuals tend to perceive other's innocuous actions as threatening; people who habitually lie seem to be more suspicious of others, and people who dislike others will often perceive that they themselves are hated. Projection has some basis in psychological science. In one experiment, participants took a personality test and were given intentionally false negative feedback about an aspect of their personalities. Next, they were asked to rate another person on the same personality traits. Participants tended to over-report the negative traits in others that they themselves scored poorly on.

5. MASLOW'S PYRAMID AND JACOB'S LADDER: FULFILLING A HIERARCHY OF NEEDS

וַיִּדַּר יַעֲקֹב נֶדֶר לֵאמֹר אִם יִהְיֶה אֱלֹקִים עִמָּדִי וּשְׁמָרַנִי בַּדֶּרֶךְ הַזֶּה אֲשֶׁר אָנֹכִי הוֹלֵךְ וְנָתַן לִי לֶחֶם לֶאֱכֹל וּבֶגֶד לִלְבֹּשׁ: וְשַׁבְתִּי בְשָׁלוֹם אֶל בֵּית אָבִי וְהָיָה ה' לִי לֵאלֹקִים.

---

[8] R. F. Baumeister, K. Dale, and K. L. Sommer, "Freudian Defense Mechanisms and Empirical Findings in Modern Social Psychology: Reaction Formation, Projection, Displacement, Undoing, Isolation, Sublimation, and Denial," *Journal of Personality* 66(6) (1998): 1090–92.

And Yaakov took an oath saying: If God will be with me, and protect me along my journey that I am traveling, and will provide bread to eat and clothing to wear, and allow me to return safely to my father's house, and be my God...

Bereishis 28:20–21

After Yaakov dreams about "a ladder set on the ground and its top reached to the sky,"[9] he makes a bargain with God and asks for basic needs such as food, clothing, and safety. It seems strange that Yaakov stipulated that he could only fulfill his promise of giving charity and proclaiming God's greatness if God provides these for him. However, there is a famous psychological concept of the hierarchy of needs, coined by Abraham Maslow, a Jewish twentieth-century psychologist, in 1943. Maslow conceptualized the way people rank their needs as a pyramid made up of different levels, prioritized from bottom to top. For instance, the most basic physiological necessities, such as food, water, and sleep, make up the base of the pyramid. The next level includes needs such as safety, security, and stability. After that comes relationship needs, such as love and belonging, followed by self-esteem goals like confidence, esteem, and achievement. Finally, the pinnacle of the pyramid is what Maslow called

---

9   *Bereishis* 28:12.

"self-actualization"—the ultimate goal of achieving one's full potential. Maslow explained that one cannot advance up the pyramid unless the needs of the lower levels are first fulfilled.[10] So when someone is in a state of crisis (e.g., displaced from home), and their basic physical needs are not guaranteed, further growth and development in higher levels becomes very challenging and of less importance. It could be that Yaakov was simply saying to God: I want to give charity and proclaim Your greatness, and I don't need to have *all* my needs met to do so, but I do need to have my basic physical needs taken care of.

---

10 A. H. Maslow, "A Theory of Human Motivation," *Psychological Review* 50(4) (1943): 370–396.

Chapter 4

ANXIETY

and

OBSESSIVE-COMPULSIVE

DISORDER

1. REAL CONCERNS VS. OBSESSIVE WORRIES

אין חוששין שמא גררה חלדה מבית לבית וממקום למקום, דאם כן, מחצר לחצר ומעיר לעיר, אין לדבר סוף.

There is no need to be concerned that a weasel may have dragged chametz from one house to another, or one location to another. For if we were to be concerned about that, what if it went from one courtyard to another? Or from one city to another? And there would be no end to the possibilities.

Mishnah, Pesachim 1:2

Obsessive worries usually take the form of "what if" questions: What if I lose my job? What if I get sick? What if other people judge me? When such concerns are realistic, it is good to ask these sorts of questions so that we can remain prepared to handle challenges. Further, asking occasional "what if" questions about life concerns can help us accept that life is uncertain, and that anything can happen. But when we worry about unrealistic fears, or even when we worry too much about realistic concerns, worrying becomes counterproductive and can be damaging to our mental health. In fact, evidence from psychological science suggests that excessively worrying about a problem can (ironically) create an illusory feeling that it is under control, which leads to worse decision making.[1] Perhaps for these reasons, *Chazal* tell us in the above Mishnah that despite the importance of removing *chametz* in preparation for the Pesach holiday, we need to consider whether our concerns are real or obsessive. *Chazal* caution us that if what we're worrying about isn't a realistic concern, we need to let go and move on, because otherwise we would simply worry forever.

Credits: Dr. Yonatan Sobin, Center for Anxiety

---

1   D. A. Worthy, K. A. Byrne, S. Fields, "Effects of Emotion on Prospection during Decision-Making," *Frontiers in Psychology* 5:591(2014), doi:10.3389/fpsyg. 2014.0059.

2. TAKING DEEP BREATHS TO COPE WITH ANXIETY

וַיְדַבֵּר מֹשֶׁה כֵּן אֶל בְּנֵי יִשְׂרָאֵל וְלֹא שָׁמְעוּ אֶל מֹשֶׁה מִקֹּצֶר רוּחַ וּמֵעֲבֹדָה קָשָׁה:

Moshe said these words to the Children of Israel, but they did not listen to Moshe because of their shortness of breath and because of their hard labor.

מִקֹּצֶר רוּחַ. כל מי שהוא מצר, רוחו ונשימתו קצרה, ואינו יכול להאריך בנשימתו.

Anyone who is in distress experiences shortness of breath and cannot breathe deeply.

Rashi to *Shemos* 6:9

Human beings are blessed with the fight-or-flight response system, which can help us survive extreme situations. When our physical safety is threatened, our sympathetic nervous system activates to create adaptive physiological changes, including a rapid heart rate (to increase flow of blood to the body), heavy breathing (to increase oxygen intake), muscle tension (to increase strength), and changes in digestion (to divert resources to survival mechanisms). Anxiety can be thought of as an oversensitive fight-or-flight system. In anxious individuals, such physiological changes occur even in response to situations that are *not* extreme or genuinely dangerous circumstances. One strategy that reduces these symptoms is diaphragmatic breathing.[2] In this approach, one sits comfortably and takes slow, deep breaths by extending their belly out with each inhalation and depressing it with each exhalation. Diaphragmatic breathing overrides the fight-or-flight response by activating the parasympathetic nervous system, which calms the body down after the threat of danger is no longer present. While this approach typically does not cure anxiety, it can be a helpful strategy for quelling symptoms.

3. SETTING ASIDE "WORRY TIME" EACH DAY TO FIGHT ANXIETY

וראוי לקבע לו איזה שעה ביום לשבר לבו ולפרש שיחתו לפניו יתברך,
כמובא אצלנו אבל כל היום כלו צריך להיות בשמחה.

It is good to set aside a specific time every day to open up one's heart to God and to tell Him what's on your mind, and this way you will [free up your mind to] be happy the rest of the day.

Rabbi Nachman of Breslov,
Likutei Moharan, vol. II, chap. 24

---

2   Y. Chen, X. Huang, C. Chien, and J. Cheng, "The Effectiveness of Diaphragmatic Breathing Relaxation Training for Reducing Anxiety," *Perspectives in Psychiatric Care* 53(4) (2017): 329–336.

In this passage, Rabbi Nachman is teaching his followers that they need not be concerned that speaking about their troubles to God will hamper the relationship. Rather, the exact opposite is true—by setting aside time each day to verbalize one's concerns, it actually helps contain those negative feelings so that they don't permeate the rest of the day. This technique of setting aside time in each day to focus on one's problems and concerns is supported by modern psychological science too. There is a common tool used in CBT to treat anxiety, called "worry time,"[3] in which patients are instructed to reserve a period of time each day to focus on worrying. Excessive worriers often complain that their anxiety is present throughout the day with no reprieve from distress. However, they are typically experiencing low-levels of unrelenting anxiety because they avoid more intense emotional experiences. Constant worry is a maladaptive way to control one's anxiety—by always being on alert and concerned, people feel they will avoid the possibility of something truly disastrous occurring.[4] For these and other reasons, worriers are encouraged to set aside "worry time" to seriously and deeply consider all that might go wrong. The

---

[3] M. G. Craske and D. H. Barlow, *Mastery of Your Anxiety and Worry* (Oxford University Press, 2006).

[4] M. H. Freeston, J. Rhéaume, H. Letarte, M. J. Dugas, and R. Ladouceur, "Why Do People Worry?" *Personality and Individual Differences* 17(6) (1994): 791–802.

experience of this method is initially very scary, but people gradually learn to face elevated levels of distress, and they often start to problem-solve their concerns instead of simply reviewing them. As an added benefit, whenever low-level anxious thoughts creep up throughout the day, they can always be postponed by saying, "I'll focus on this during my worry time."

4. THE APPROACH-AVOIDANCE CONFLICT: LEAN IN TO YOUR ANXIETIES

ויגש. ההקרבה למלך וגדול או למקום סכנה נקראה הגשה.

He approached (va'yigash): The root word "gash" is used when someone approaches a king or superior, or dangerous situation.

Hakesav Vehakabalah to Bereishis 18:23

ויאמרו גש הלאה. קרב להלאה, כלומר, התקרב לצדדין והתרחק ממנו, וכן כל הלאה שבמקרא לשון רחוק.

And they said, "Go close (gash) to over there (hallah)": Which means to go to the sides, for the word "hallah" means to distance oneself.

Rashi to Bereishis 19:9

The Torah includes many narratives of individuals faced with great dilemmas who can choose either to approach or to avoid difficult situations.[5] Courageously facing the danger is represented with the word *gash*, which means to draw close, and implies more than a physical proximity—a willingness to confront a situation head-on. Interestingly, in the *Rashi* quoted above, the verse uses the word *gash* in an instance of someone creating distance, the opposite of *gash*. When *gash* is followed by the word *hallah*, it conveys a sense of creating distance, which could also imply a form of avoidance. This contradictory nature of the Hebrew word couple is reminiscent of the approach-avoidance conflict, an important psychological concept. When someone is faced with an opportunity that has both positive and negative ramifications (e.g., a new job offer, partnership, or serious relationship), they often feel stressed about making a decision.[6] The excitement and potential gain of approaching the situation tend to be more dominant initially, creating positive feelings, but as it becomes closer to a reality (e.g., the day of the wedding), negative feelings increase and avoidance is stronger. Research suggests that the best approach to overcoming anxiety is to face your fears and follow through, because avoidance tends to reinforce anxiety and only make it worse in the future. A popular expression says to "lean in" to difficult

---

5   See also the story of Yehudah and Yosef, *Bereishis* 44:18.
6   K. Lewin, *A Dynamic Theory of Personality* (New York: McGraw-Hill, 1935).

Anxiety and Obsessive-Compulsive Disorder

conversations, debates, and interactions in order to spur healthy communication and change.[7]

5. DOUBT, UNCERTAINTY, AND CHOICE OVERLOAD

אין בעולם שמחה כהתרת הספקות.

There is no greater joy in the world than resolving doubt.

Metzudas David, Mishlei 15:30

Feelings of uncertainty can be unpleasant at best and paralyzing at worst. Whether we fear a future outcome (e.g., an exam or medical test results) or cannot predict the optimal outcome of a decision, most individuals, especially those with anxiety, have difficulty coping with doubt. In fact, some researchers believe that the steady decline in mental well-being in society, even while all other quality of life metrics improve, is due to "choice overload," which refers to a phenomenon that arises when a large array of options or choices overwhelms one's critical faculties, creating anxiety and decreasing satisfaction.[8] Many studies have shown that when individuals are offered a surfeit of choices, rather than making them feel fortunate for having many options, this actually distresses

---

[7] S. Sandberg, *Lean In: Women, Work, and the Will to Lead* (New York: Alfred A. Knopf, 2013).

[8] Robert E. Lane, *The Loss of Happiness in Market Economies* (New Haven, CT: Yale University Press, 2000).

them by making their decisions difficult.[9] Negative emotions such as disappointment and regret are also more prevalent when there are more options to begin with.[10] One method that the Torah prescribes to help overcome this problem is a system of decision heuristics. In halachah, there are infinite situations of doubt in terms of the proper course of action or status of an item. Yet, rather than attempt to clarify the objective facts of the situation, the Jewish legal system will often resolve the conflict based on a set of priority rules. For instance, when someone is presented with the opportunity to perform only one of two mitzvos due to time constraints, the mitzvah that will expire more quickly (i.e., *mitzvah overes*) takes precedence.[11] Therefore, if someone is suffering from choice overload, the solution is to prioritize urgent tasks first. This helps resolve conflicts with minimal mental exhaustion.

6. CHRONIC ANXIETY CAN CAUSE PHYSICAL HEALTH PROBLEMS

שלשה דברים מכחישים כחו של אדם ואלו הן: פחד, דרך, ועון. פחד
דכתיב (תהלים לח, יא) לבי סחרחר עזבני כחי.

---

9   Sheena S. Iyengar and Mark R. Lepper, "When Choice Is Demotivating: Can One Desire Too Much of a Good Thing?" *Journal of Personality and Social Psychology* 79(6) (2000): 995–1006.

10 Barry Schwartz, "Self-Determination: The Tyranny of Freedom," *American Psychologist* 55 (1) (2000): 79–88.

11 *Talmud Bavli, Berachos* 27a, *Kiddushin* 29b.

Three things weaken a person's strength: Fear, traveling on a journey, and sin. Fear, as it is written: "My heart flutters, my strength leaves me" (Tehillim 38:11).

Talmud Bavli, Gittin 70a

This Talmudic passage teaches us a truth that is widely known in psychological science today: In addition to its psychological symptoms, anxiety can cause physical ailments as well. Symptoms such as rapid heart rate, chest pain, dizziness, and nausea without a known medical cause are common reasons that people are referred to psychotherapy by their primary care providers.[12] This is especially true among children, who do not have the developmental capacity to be fully aware of their anxiety and therefore tend to express symptoms somatically. The effects of chronic stress and anxiety can be devastating, as they can potentially lead to a weakened immune system and long-term health problems such as stomach ulcers and heart disease.[13] This is because stress and anxiety activate the body's fight-or-flight response system, which pumps adrenaline and cortisol into the blood stream. These hormones increase heart rate,

---

12 T. A. Stern and J. B. Herman, eds., *Massachusetts General Hospital Psychiatry Update and Board Preparation* (McGraw-Hill, 1999), 395–419.

13 A. M. Roest, E. J. Martens, P. de Jonge, and J. Denollet, "Anxiety and Risk of Incident Coronary Heart Disease: A Meta-Analysis," *Journal of the American College of Cardiology* 56(1) (2010): 38–46.

blood pressure, and blood sugar levels and suppress a host of systems including immune, digestive, and reproductive functioning. Therefore, psychological interventions such as CBT have been found to be highly effective in reducing symptoms associated with health problems. For instance, a review of studies conducted with children and adolescents with chronic illness found that psychotherapy was equally as effective as disease management interventions.[14]

7. TRUST IN GOD CAN HELP WITH WORRY

אך תועלות הבטחון בעולם...והוא בהשקט ובבטחה ובשלוה בעולם הזה.

One of the benefits of trust in God is...serenity, feeling secure and at peace in this world.

Duties of the Heart,
"Gate of Trust in God," introduction

A substantial body of evidence indicates that anxiety in general, and worry in particular, stems from the inability to tolerate an uncertain future.[15] The above quotation thus

---

14   M. Y. Kibby, V. L. Tyc, and R. K. Mulhern, "Effectiveness of Psychological Intervention for Children and Adolescents with Chronic Medical Illness: A Meta-Analysis," *Clinical Psychology Review* 18(1) (1998): 103–17.

15   M. J. Dugas, K. Buhr, and R. Ladouceur, "The Role of Intolerance of Uncertainty in Etiology and Maintenance," in R. G. Heimberg, C. L. Turk, and D. S. Mennin, eds., *Generalized Anxiety Disorder: Advances in Research and Practice* (New York: Guilford Press, 2004), 143–163.

provides a potential solution: by maintaining awareness that God is in control and that ultimately what God does is for the best, one can embrace uncertainty and overcome worry. Based on this concept, over the past decade a number of psychological studies have examined the relationship between trust in God and worry. Findings have indicated that both Jewish and non-Jewish individuals who report greater trust in God have significantly less worry and stress, as well as greater levels of happiness and enjoyment of life.[16] It seems that greater trust in God predicts greater ability to tolerate uncertain life events, which in turn alleviates worry.[17] Furthermore, a randomized controlled trial, with 125 individuals engaging in a brief two-week web-based program entitled "Increase Your Trust in God," yielded substantial reductions in worry, stress, and depression, and

---

16   D. H. Rosmarin, K. I. Pargament, and A. Mahoney, "The Role of Religiousness in Anxiety, Depression, and Happiness in a Jewish Community Sample: A Preliminary Investigation," *Mental Health, Religion and Culture* 12(2) (2009): 97–113. See also D. H. Rosmarin, E. J. Krumrei, and G. Andersson, "Religion as a Predictor of Psychological Distress in Two Religious Communities," *Cognitive Behaviour Therapy* 38(1) (2009): 54–64.

17   D. H. Rosmarin, S. Pirutinsky, R. P. Auerbach, T. Björgvinsson, J. Bigda-Peyton, G. Andersson, and E. J. Krumrei, "Incorporating Spiritual Beliefs into a Cognitive Model of Worry," *Journal of Clinical Psychology* 67(7) (2011): 691–700.

was more effective than a more commonly utilized secular approach (progressive muscle relaxation).[18]

---

[18] D. H. Rosmarin, K. I. Pargament, S. Pirutinsky, and A. Mahoney, "A Randomized Controlled Evaluation of a Spiritually Integrated Treatment for Subclinical Anxiety in the Jewish Community, Delivered via the Internet," *Journal of Anxiety Disorders* 24(7) (2010): 799–808.

Chapter 5

DEPRESSION

1. SCHEDULING PLEASANT ACTIVITIES TO HELP WITH DEPRESSION

אם תתעורר עליו לחה שחורה יסירה בשמיעת הניגונים ובמיני זמר, והטיול בגינות והבניינים הנאים, וחברת הצורות היפות וכיוצא בזה ממה שירחיב הנפש ויסור המרה השחורה ממנה.

One who suffers from melancholia may rid himself of it by listening to songs and instrumental music, by strolling through gardens and magnificent buildings, frequenting attractive works of art, and other things that broaden the spirit, and in this way help to dissipate the sense of gloom that has overcome him.

Rambam, *Shemoneh Perakim* 5:2

Here, the *Rambam* suggests a treatment approach for depression that is widely practiced today. Psychological research has shown that depressed individuals often experience a combination of lack of enjoyment (anhedonia) and sadness (dysphoria), and these two core symptoms seem to be closely intertwined in the structure of the brain.[1] In fact, neuroimaging studies with depressed individuals have specifically found a decreased pleasure experience during basic recreational activities, such as listening to music.[2] For this reason, one strategy for overcoming depression is to simply schedule and engage in fulfilling and prosocial activities (even if they are not initially pleasurable).[3] This approach is highly effective at treating depression because it changes neural activity such that it becomes easier to experience positive feelings and enjoyment over time.[4]

Credits: Rabbi Yechezkel Nulman, Kollel of Greater Boston

---

[1] K. C. Berridge and M. L. Kringelbach, "Pleasure Systems in the Brain," *Neuron* 86(3) (2015): 646–664.

[2] E. A. Osuch, R. L. Bluhm, P. C. Williamson, J. Theberge, M. Densmore, and R. W. Neufeld, "Brain Activation to Favorite Music in Healthy Controls and Depressed Patients," *Neuroreport* 20(13) (2009): 1204–1208.

[3] P. Cuijpers, A. Van Straten, and L. Warmerdam, "Behavioral Activation Treatments of Depression: A Meta-Analysis," *Clinical Psychology Review* 27(3) (2007): 318–326.

[4] M. J. Gawrysiak, J. P. Carvalho, B. P. Rogers, C. R. N. Nicholas, J. H. Dougherty, and D. R. Hopko, "Neural Changes following Behavioral Activation for a Depressed Breast Cancer Patient: A Functional MRI Case Study," *Case Reports in Psychiatry*.

2. THE CYCLICAL NATURE OF DEPRESSION

אולם, ידיעה זו לבדה, כי התחלפות ימי האהבה וימי השנאה דבר טבעי
הוא – בכוחה להפיג הרבה מן היאוש והעצבות.

The very awareness of the fact that it is natural to have good days and bad days has the power to alleviate much of one's despair and sadness.

Rabbi Shlomo Wolbe, *Alei Shur*, Vol. I, p. 35

This passage teaches the importance of accepting emotional highs and lows as an essential part of life. When people enter a depressed state, they often wonder why they are feeling sad and if it will ever go away. Here, Rav Wolbe teaches us a tried-and-tested principle of CBT: emotions are cyclical. Even the happiest people have sad days. Therefore, the experience of sadness in and of itself is no cause for deeper sadness or despair. On the contrary, feeling sad at times only means that you are human, and is nothing to feel guilty, confused, or frustrated about. In many cases, one can detect trends and identify triggers that initiate or maintain depressive episodes. However, studies show that excessively pondering the causes, meanings, and consequences of depressed moods tends to make things worse by increasing negative thinking and symptoms of depression.[5]

---

5   L. M. Rubenstein, J. L. Hamilton, J. P. Stange, M. Flynn, L. Y. Abramson, and L. B. Alloy, "The Cyclical Nature of Depressed Mood and Future Risk:

This concept points to another important principle: the best approach to take when one is feeling sad is to accept the "bad days" as par for the course, and remain engaged and active until the "good days" return. This is because mood states don't last forever—they ebb and flow, and sometimes one just has to ride it out.

Credits: Rabbi Ben Geiger, Los Angeles, CA

3. PASSIVE SUICIDAL IDEATION: COPING WITH SERIOUS EMOTIONAL PAIN

וַיֵּרַע אֶל יוֹנָה רָעָה גְדוֹלָה וַיִּחַר לוֹ...וְעַתָּה ה' קַח נָא אֶת נַפְשִׁי מִמֶּנִּי כִּי טוֹב מוֹתִי מֵחַיָּי.

Yonah experienced incredible distress and he was distraught...and said, "Please God, take away my life, for I'd rather be dead than alive."

Yonah 4:1, 3

Although one must be extremely careful when analyzing the character traits of our great prophets, lest they misinterpret their true meaning, the Torah often highlights the struggles of holy individuals in order to teach us valuable lessons. On the most mundane level, the content of Yonah's thoughts and speech seem similar in tone to many individuals

---

Depression, Rumination, and Deficits in Emotional Clarity in Adolescent Girls," *Journal of Adolescence* 42 (2015): 68–76.

who are depressed. One of the symptoms of depression is "recurrent thoughts of death, recurrent suicidal ideation."[6] Suicidal ideation refers to having thoughts about dying. These thoughts can be divided into two categories: active and passive.[7] Active ideation is when an individual is contemplating how to engage in specific suicide methods, and perhaps even devises a plan of action. With active suicidal ideation, depressed individuals may even begin to research methods of killing themselves or write a suicide note. Active ideation is extremely concerning and immediate intervention is warranted. However, much more often, suicidal thoughts are passive and simply involve thoughts or feelings that one would be better off dead. These latter feelings are very common when people are experiencing great distress. Hearing people say things such as "I wish I were dead," "I want to go to sleep and not wake up," or "I hope the world ends tomorrow," may sound terrifying to the individual and their loved ones, but such statements do not necessarily mean the individual

---

[6] American Psychiatric Association, *Diagnostic and Statistical Manual of Mental Disorders*, 5th ed. (Arlington, VA: American Psychiatric Publishing, 2013).

[7] A. T. Beck, M. Kovacs, and A. Weissman, "Assessment of Suicidal Intention: The Scale for Suicide Ideation," *Journal of Consulting and Clinical Psychology* 47(2) (1979): 343.

is actually suicidal or at risk.[8] Rather, such thoughts could be a coping strategy (albeit a poor one)—to wish it would all go away—when faced with a seemingly insurmountable burden of emotional pain. This should be seen as a cry for help and should be met with support as well as psychotherapy.

4. RELIGIOUS PRACTICE WITHOUT BELIEF CAN WORSEN DEPRESSION

חובות האברים לא תשלמנה כי אם ברצון הלב וחפץ הנפש לעשותם ותאות לבנו לפעול אותם...מפני שאין מעשה נשלם מבלי חפץ הנפש בו.

The physical obligations (i.e., action-based mitzvos) cannot be performed properly unless they are paired with intent, consciousness, and emotional desire to perform them...for no act can be complete without the agreement of the soul.

Duties of the Heart, author's introduction

In this section, the *Chovos Halevavos* elaborates on the supreme importance of "internal processes" such as belief, values, and commitment with regard to religious practice. It also warns of the shallowness associated with meaningless

---

8   R. C. Kessler, G. Borges, and E. E. Walters, "Prevalence of and Risk Factors for Lifetime Suicide Attempts in the National Comorbidity Survey," *Archives of General Psychiatry* 56(7), (1999): 617–626.

observance. Besides the moral implications of this imperative, lack of belief leads to detrimental effects on an individual's mental well-being. A recent study examined the relationship between the severity of mood disorders in Jewish individuals measured against their religious observance and general attitudes. There were 160 participants, sixty percent of whom identified as Orthodox-Jewish, with diagnoses of depression or bipolar disorder. They were asked questions regarding their intrinsic religiosity as well as their religious practice. Participants who endorsed high religious practice but low intrinsic religiosity were significantly more likely to become more depressed over time, whereas those that endorsed high intrinsic religiosity were more likely to become less depressed.[9]

5. FINDING MEANING HELPS OVERCOME GRIEF

וַיִּנָּחֶם ה' כִּי עָשָׂה אֶת הָאָדָם בָּאָרֶץ וַיִּתְעַצֵּב אֶל לִבּוֹ.

And Hashem regretted that He created man on the earth, and He felt grief in His heart.

Bereishis 6:6

דבר אחר וַיִּנָּחֶם—נהפכה מחשבתו של מקום...וכן כל לשון נחום שבמקרא לשון נמלך...כלם לשון מחשבה אחרת הם.

---

[9] S. Pirutinsky and D. H. Rosmarin, "Protective and Harmful Effects of Religious Practice on Depression among Jewish Individuals with Mood Disorders," *Clinical Psychological Science* (2018): 2167702617748402.

> *"And Hashem was consoled" means that God changed His mind...Wherever the term "consoled" is used in Tanach, it means "reconsidering"...All those instances denote a change of mind.*
>
> Rashi, Bereishis 6:6

Although the Hebrew word *nechamah* is often translated to mean "comfort" or "consolation," a more accurate meaning is "a change in perspective." Taken a step further, Rabbi Samson Raphael Hirsch explains that developing a positive reframing on tragic events is a healthy path toward comfort and emotional healing.[10] This concept is well established in the clinical treatment of trauma and grief. One of the most effective methods for helping individuals who have suffered a loss is known as "meaning-making," which is the process of making sense of life events and constructing a renewed sense of purpose.[11] Conversely, psychological research has shown that the inability to find meaning following a traumatic event usually prevents grief from resolving over time.[12]

---

10 Commentary to *Bereishis* 5:30.

11 C. L. Park, "Making Sense of the Meaning Literature: An Integrative Review of Meaning Making and Its Effects on Adjustment to Stressful Life Events," *Psychological Bulletin* 136(2) (2010): 257.

12 J. M. Currier, J. M. Holland, and R. A. Neimeyer, "Sense-Making, Grief, and the Experience of Violent Loss: Toward a Mediational Model," *Death Studies* 30(5) (2006): 403–428.

Chapter 6

PARENTING

1. A UNIFIED VOICE IN THE HOME IMPROVES CHILD BEHAVIORS

כִּי יִהְיֶה לְאִישׁ בֵּן סוֹרֵר וּמוֹרֶה אֵינֶנּוּ שֹׁמֵעַ בְּקוֹל אָבִיו וּבְקוֹל אִמּוֹ וְיִסְּרוּ אֹתוֹ וְלֹא יִשְׁמַע אֲלֵיהֶם.

If a man has a wayward and defiant son, who does not obey his father's voice, nor his mother's voice, and does not obey them even after they discipline him...

Devarim 21:18

[O]nly if both father and mother exercise their educative influence on him, and if the father and mother have one voice, both treat him with the same seriousness, both stand over him in equal authority, in equal dignity, and above all, in the same agreed ideas and wishes, only then can they say to themselves that it is not their fault if their son is a failure. If any one of these factors is missing, where, above all, there

> *is not complete agreement between the parents in bringing up their children, then the failure of the child is no proof of the moral badness of his nature. Under a truly better system of education on the part of the father and mother, the child might perhaps have been different.*
>
> Rabbi Samson Raphael Hirsch,
> Commentary to *Devarim* 21:18[1]

In stating that the defiant son does not listen to his parents, the verse uses two separate phrases ("his father's voice" and "his mother's voice"), suggesting that a child's father's and mother's voices are dissimilar—and perhaps even contradictory. The Torah is teaching us that when parents send conflicting messages to a child, it can be confusing to the child and can cause him to act out in a way that is "wayward and rebellious."[2] This concept is well established within modern psychological science. Children—in particular, adolescents—who are given inconsistent messages from their parents are susceptible to developing defiant attitudes and to questioning authority. In one recent study, inconsistent discipline strategies between parents was a stronger predictor of behavioral problems

---

1 See also *Orchos Yosher* by Rav Chaim Kanievsky, p. 38.
2 *Talmud Bavli, Sanhedrin* 71a.

than any other parenting variable.[3] To this end, the most effective parenting-based therapies today, such as Parent-Child Interaction Therapy, Parent Management Training, and Behavioral Parent Training, all strongly emphasize that parents must be on the same page when instructing children.[4]

2. A HEALTHY MARRIAGE PROMOTES CHILDREN'S SPIRITUAL DEVELOPMENT

שְׁלָחַיִךְ פַּרְדֵּס רִמּוֹנִים עִם פְּרִי מְגָדִים.

Your arid fields are as a pomegranate orchard with sweet fruit.

Shir Hashirim 4:13

ועולימיך מלין פקודין הכרימונין ורחמין לנשיהון וילדן בנין צדיקין כותהון.

Your young men are full of mitzvos like pomegranates (are filled with seeds), and they adore their wives and beget children righteous as themselves.

Targum Yonasan

---

[3] P. J. Frick, R. E. Christian, and J. M. Wootton (1999), "Age trends in the association between parenting practices and conduct problems," *Behavior Modification* 23(1), 106–128.

[4] S. M. Eyeberg, M. M. Nelson, and S. R. Boggs (2008), "Evidence-based psychosocial treatments for children and adolescents with disruptive behavior," *Journal of Clinical Child and Adolescent Psychology* 37(1), 215–237.

ואוהבים את נשותיהם ויולדים משום כך צדיקים.

*The men adore their wives, and **for this reason** have righteous children.*

Meoros Hamegillah *commentary to* Targum Yonasan

This source states the opinion that the most important ingredient to raising righteous and upstanding children is not primarily a solid religious education but a healthy marriage. It is widely known that marital conflict can engender behavioral problems in children (see previous entry above). But many parents make the error of focusing solely on what they see is best for their children without examining what is best for their relationship as a couple. Modern psychological science has highlighted that marital matrimony and unification are more important factors than a host of other factors in predicting the well-being of children.[5] Furthermore, and more directly related to the above source, religious and spiritual development of children is better predicted by marital relationship factors than religious education and other aspects of upbringing.[6] One explanation for this is as follows: Marital harmony requires putting one's own needs

---

5   S. Y. Kwok, L. Cheng, B. W. Chow, and C. C. Ling, "The Spillover Effect of Parenting on Marital Satisfaction among Chinese Mothers," *Journal of Child and Family Studies* 24(3) (2015): 772–783.

6   C. J. Boyatzis, D. C. Dollahite, and L. D. Marks, "The Family as a Context for Religious and Spiritual Development in Children and Youth,"

and wants aside for the sake of the other (i.e., selflessness). This process mimics the internal choreography that is necessary for religious development: spiritual growth requires appraising God's "wants" and giving those priority over one's own preferences. In these respects, the best preparation for spiritual growth is enhancing the quality of our interpersonal relationships, starting with the most fundamental one—our marriage.

Credits: Rabbi Tzvi Solomon, Boston, MA

3. THE RAMBAM'S TOKEN ECONOMY: REWARDING CHILDREN WITH PRIZES

ולפיכך בהכרח יצטרך המלמד שהוא יותר שלם ממנו שיזרז אותו על הלמוד בדברים שהם אהובים אצלו לקטנות שניו ויאמר לו קרא ואתן לך אגוזים או תאנים ואתן לך מעט דבש, ובזה הוא קורא ומשתדל לא לעצם הקריאה לפי שאינו יודע מעלתה אלא כדי שיתנו לו אותו המאכל ואכילת אותן המגדים אצלו יקר בעיניו מן הקריאה וטוב הרבה בלא ספק ולפיכך חושב הלימוד עמל ויגיעה והוא עמל בו כדי שיגיע לו באותו עמל התכלית האהוב אצלו.

Therefore, it is necessary for the teacher, who has more understanding, to encourage the child to study with things that the child likes due to his immaturity. The

---

The Handbook of Spiritual Development in Childhood and Adolescence (2006): 297–309.

> teacher should say "Read, and I will give you nuts or figs, or I will give you a little honey." This will motivate the child to read and exert himself—not for the actual learning, for it is not valuable to him, but rather for the food. Without a doubt, the treats are more precious in his eyes than the reading and intrinsic value. Though he views the study as work and a struggle; he tries so that he will be rewarded.
>
> Rambam, introduction to *Perek Chelek*

Here the *Rambam* describes the tried-and-tested method of using positive reinforcement to shape behaviors in children—and even adolescents and adults. This approach, known as "token economy," is standard in almost all evidence-based treatments for childhood disorders and can be highly effective in motivating children to engage in otherwise difficult tasks. Interestingly, parents often have reservations about using external, tangible rewards to reinforce their children. They expect that children should be intrinsically motivated to behave, and they are often resistant to rewarding children for actions that are expected of them (e.g., household chores, homework, or sharing). In almost all cases, especially with young children, this is not a realistic expectation, and withholding token reinforcers can cause significant family distress in many cases. More importantly, a frequent concern among parents is that the child will only be motivated to obtain the reward, and the intrinsic value of the task will not be internalized.[7] The *Rambam* preemptively addresses these issues by highlighting the developmental appropriateness of this method and by explaining that the goal of establishing good habits is achievable through rewards. As children's intellectual capacities develop, external rewards should be modified and substituted accordingly, so that the same tasks will eventually become more intrinsically motivating.

4. BREAKING OUT OF THE COERCIVE CYCLE IN PARENTING

> *Train yourself to endure his outbursts of impatience or his temper tantrums, so that you should not, out of a selfish desire for some peace and quiet, grant your child a wish that you would otherwise deny him…above all, he must never be…allowed to think that if he torments and annoys you sufficiently, he can get you to permit what you originally forbade him.*
>
> Rabbi Samson Raphael Hirsch[8]

---

7   A. Kohn, *Punished by Rewards: The Trouble with Gold Stars, Incentive Plans, A's, Praise, and Other Bribes* (Boston, MA: Houghton Mifflin, 1999).
8   "On the Role of Education in the First Years of a Child's Life," included in the *Collected Writings of Rabbi Samson Raphael Hirsch*, vol. 7 (Jerusalem: Feldheim, 1997), p. 132.

Writing in the mid-nineteenth century, Rav Hirsch here describes an important parent-child dynamic that is today a cornerstone of treatment for oppositional and defiant children. Not giving in to tantrums is an established practice in clinical science for virtually all childhood disruptive behavior disorders. This is because the parent-child relationship is critical to the outcome of children's behavioral issues. Gerald Patterson, a "forefather" of modern-day parent training psychotherapy, described a process in parent-child relations know as a "coercive cycle."[9] As Patterson observed, parents and children often fall into relational cycles that reinforce maladaptive behaviors of both parties. For instance, when a parent denies a request of a child, the child is likely to engage in disruptive behaviors such as tantrums in order to achieve their goal. It is understandable that a parent would naturally wish to avoid the child's negative and disruptive reaction, especially in public, so the parent may acquiesce to the child's wish, leading the child to temporarily calm down. Although the parent experiences short-term relief, they have inadvertently rewarded the child's behavior, making it more likely to reoccur. Over time, these patterns of interaction become ingrained and very difficult to reverse unless parents receive coaching to learn more effective strategies.

---

9   G. R. Patterson, "The Aggressive Child: Victim and Architect of a Coercive System," *Behavior Modification and Families* 1 (1976): 267–316.

5. EFFECTIVE PARENTING BEGINS WITH REDUCING COMMANDS

Be reasonable, circumspect, and sparing with commands and prohibitions. Never give your child orders that are unnecessary or unimportant. Think carefully before you issue a command to your child.

Rabbi Samson Raphael Hirsch[10]

In this excerpt, Rav Hirsch emphasizes another parenting technique that is a major component of effective parent training treatments for young children. Parents often fail to realize how often they give commands to their children, and how infrequently children actually comply. This is ineffective for two reasons. First, parents end up training their children to ignore their commands, and second, children become bombarded with commands, which is both unpleasant and unlikely to lead to compliance. Therefore, parent-training protocols such as Parent-Child Interaction Therapy (PCIT) coach parents to reduce commands, to only use verbal cues when necessary, and to focus attention on getting children to comply with fewer requests.[11] In a five-minute window, the optimal frequency

---

10 "On the Role of Education in the First Years of a Child's Life," included in the *Collected Writings of Rabbi Samson Raphael Hirsch*, vol. 7 (Jerusalem: Feldheim, 1997), p. 132.

11 T. L. Hembree-Kigin, and C. B. McNeil, *Parent-Child Interaction Therapy* (Springer Science and Business Media, 2013).

is about one command per minute with young children. Not only does this train children to better notice and take heed of their parents' requests, it also leads to improvements in the parent-child relationship; since commands create opportunities for power struggles, especially with oppositional children, reducing commands limits the potential for conflict.

6. BEDTIME ROUTINES IMPROVE SLEEP

ברוך אתה ה' אלהינו מלך העולם המפיל חבלי שינה על עיני ותנומה
על עפעפי, ויהי רצון מלפניך ה' אלקי ואלקי אבותי, שתשכיבני לשלום
ותעמידני לשלום, ואל יבהלוני רעיוני וחלומות רעים והרהורים רעים
ותהא מיטתי שלמה לפניך, והאר עיני פן אישן המות,כי אתה המאיר
לאישון בת עין. ברוך אתה ה' המאיר לעולם כלו בכבודו.

Praised are You, Lord our God, King of the universe, who brings sleep to my eyes, slumber to my eyelids. May it be Your will, Lord my God and God of my ancestors, that I lie down in peace and that I arise in peace. Let my sleep be undisturbed by troubling thoughts, bad dreams, and wicked schemes. May I have a night of tranquil slumber. May I awaken to the light of a new day, that my eyes may behold the splendor of Your light. Praised are You, Lord whose glory gives light to the entire world.

"The Bedtime Blessing," Ashkenazic siddur[12]

---

12 *Siddur Sim Shalom: A Prayerbook for Shabbat, Festivals and Weekdays* (1985), p. 245.

This blessing is traditionally recited before going to sleep. There are additional prayers included in the ritual, and many Jewish parents have the custom of singing special prayers of protection to their children as part of their bedtime routine. This age-old custom is perhaps the first formulated bedtime routine. While modern psychological science has yet to study the effects of religious vs. non-religious approaches to the bedtime process, researchers have consistently observed positive effects of a bedtime routine on children's mental health. Anywhere from twenty to thirty percent of children experience sleep problems, and it is one of the most common concerns among parents.[13] A highly recommended treatment among pediatricians is for parents to establish regular bedtime routines with children.[14] Studies have found many benefits of children's bedtime routines, including less sleep disruption, longer total sleep time, and even improved daytime behaviors.[15] One particularly interesting study found

---

13   J. A. Mindell, B. Kuhn, and D. S. Lewin, "Erratum: Behavioral Treatment of Bedtime Problems and Night Wakings in Infants and Young Children," *Sleep* 29(10) (2006): 1263–1276.

14   J. A. Mindell, M. L. Moline, S. M. Zendell, L. W. Brown, and J. M. Fry, "Pediatricians and Sleep Disorders: Training and Practice," *Pediatrics* 94(2) (1994): 194–200.

15   C. Koulouglioti, R. Cole, M. Moskow, B. McQuillan, M. A. Carno, and A. Grape, "The Longitudinal Association of Young Children's Everyday Routines to Sleep Duration," *Journal of Pediatric Health Care* 28(1) (2014): 80–87.

that language-based routines that include singing, reading and/or story telling lead to lasting, long-term benefits on child sleep and even cognitive development.[16]

7. CORPORAL PUNISHMENT IS POOR MODELING AND EMOTIONALLY DAMAGING TO CHILDREN

וַיְדַבֵּר ה' אֶל מֹשֶׁה לֵּאמֹר: קַח אֶת הַמַּטֶּה וְהַקְהֵל אֶת הָעֵדָה אַתָּה וְאַהֲרֹן אָחִיךָ וְדִבַּרְתֶּם אֶל הַסֶּלַע לְעֵינֵיהֶם וְנָתַן מֵימָיו וְהוֹצֵאתָ לָהֶם מַיִם מִן הַסֶּלַע וְהִשְׁקִיתָ אֶת הָעֵדָה וְאֶת בְּעִירָם... וַיָּרֶם מֹשֶׁה אֶת יָדוֹ וַיַּךְ אֶת הַסֶּלַע בְּמַטֵּהוּ פַּעֲמָיִם וַיֵּצְאוּ מַיִם רַבִּים וַתֵּשְׁתְּ הָעֵדָה וּבְעִירָם:

God spoke to Moshe saying: Take your staff and assemble the people, together with Aharon. You shall speak to the rock as they watch, and it will provide water for them. Then the people and their flock will be able to drink...Moshe lifted his hand and struck the rock with his staff; water gushed out of the rock and the people and their flock drank.

Bamidbar 20:7–8, 11

There is one critical difference between slaves and free human beings. Slaves respond to orders. Free people

---

16 L. Hale, L. M. Berger, M. K. LeBourgeois, and J. Brooks-Gunn, "A Longitudinal Study of Preschoolers' Language-Based Bedtime Routines, Sleep Duration, and Well-Being," *Journal of Family Psychology* 25(3) (2011): 423.

do not. They must be educated, informed, instructed, taught—for if not, they will not learn to take responsibility. Slaves understand that a stick is used for striking. That is how slave-masters compel obedience. Indeed, that was Moses' first encounter with his people, when he saw an Egyptian beating an Israelite. But free human beings must not be struck. They respond not to power but persuasion. They need to be spoken to.

Rabbi Lord Jonathan Sacks,
Covenant and Conversation: Chukat, 5773

In his brilliant explanation of Moshe's sin of hitting the rock instead of speaking to it,[17] Rabbi Sacks differentiates between the old-fashioned "slave" mentality of the previous generation and the new "freedom" mentality of the younger generations. Whereas the Jewish People of the older generation were ex-slaves who responded most to fear-tactics, strict orders, and harsh punishment, the children born in the desert, who had never experienced hardship, required soft verbal discipline with appropriate explanations. In the present day as well, parents raised in old-fashioned households sometimes have difficulty managing children of the millennial generation, who require more patience and rationalizations. An overwhelming

---

17 See *Bamidbar* 20:8–12 and *Shemos* 17:6.

abundance of research on corporal punishment of children (such as spanking) has found it not only to be ineffective but incredibly damaging to the long-term emotional and mental well-being of children.[18] Children who are hit by their parents internalize the message that physical force is an effective way to control others, making them more likely to exhibit violence and aggression with their peers. Parents who have difficulty managing their children's behaviors are strongly encouraged to seek professional help to learn effective parenting techniques.

8. AUTHORITATIVE PARENTING STYLE: BLENDING CHESSED AND GEVURAH MAKES TIFERES

> *Chessed [is]...giving without bounds; being unrestrained, being unbounded, and perhaps even undisciplined...Gevurah relates to barriers. Gevurah-restraint is then the opposite of Chessed-love...totally structured and restrained, within very narrow limitations. In interpersonal relationships of chessed and gevurah, if one person relates to another with chessed, he could pour out his most personal feelings.*

---

[18] B. L. Smith, "The Case against Spanking: Physical Discipline Is Slowly Declining as Some Studies Reveal Lasting Harms for Children," *Monitor on Psychology* (43)4 (April 2012). Retrieved from http://www.apa.org/monitor/2012/04/spanking.aspx.

If he related to his friend with din [gevurah], however, his relationship with him would become totally structured and restrained, within very narrow limitations. Tiferes is usually translated as "beauty," but it does not carry the usual connotation of beauty. Tiferes-beauty is like harmony, a harmonic beauty. Tiferes means you are able to harmonize and blend these two extremes. Tiferes-beauty is the balance.

Rabbi Aryeh Kaplan,
Inner Space, pp. 61–63

In his easily discernible style, Rabbi Aryeh Kaplan often uses understandable and relatable examples in his description of the Kabbalistic *sefiros*. Here, he describes different personality traits associated with *chessed* (giving), *gevurah* (strict discipline) and *tiferes* (balance). A person with a *chessed* personality type tends to be overly permissive, forgiving, and generous with others—a noble trait in moderation, but damaging in excess. On the other end of the spectrum, *gevurah*-type personalities tend to be overly strict, unforgiving, and minimally emotive. *Tiferes* represents a harmonious balance between the two, which is considered the healthiest approach. This idea is reminiscent of Diana Baumrind's well-known theory of the three parenting styles: authoritarian, permissive, and authoritative.[19] Authoritarian (*gevurah*) parents tend to be highly demanding, but unresponsive to children's emotional needs. They use corporal punishment more frequently and are primarily concerned with their child's obedience. This style is associated with negative long-term effects in children, such as depression and poor emotion regulation skills.[20] Permissive (*chessed*) parents tend to be undemanding but responsive. They typically have low expectations for child behavior and lax discipline measures, but are also emotionally nurturing. Their children are likely to exhibit poor impulse control and engage in substance use and other risky behaviors later in life.[21] Finally, authoritative (*tiferes*) parents are both demanding and supportive of their children. They enforce firm behavioral boundaries but also foster independence, problem solving, and emotional intelligence. Their children tend to become well-adjusted and self-sufficient.[22]

---

19 D. Baumrind, "Child Care Practices Anteceding Three Patterns of Preschool Behavior," *Genetic Psychology Monographs* 75(1) (1967): 43–88.

20 S. D. Lamborn, N. S. Mounts, L. Steinberg, and S. M. Dornbusch, "Patterns of Competence and Adjustment among Adolescents from Authoritative, Authoritarian, Indulgent, and Neglectful Families," *Child Development* 62(5) (1991): 1049–1065.

21 Ibid.

22 D. Baumrind, "The influence of parenting style on adolescent competence and substance use," *The Journal of Early Adolescence* 11(1) (1991), 56–95.

9. EDUCATION IS A PREPARATION FOR LIFE

והוא לשון התחלת כניסת האדם או כלי לאמנות שהוא עתיד לעמוד בה.

The word chinuch (education) refers to the initiation of an individual or utensil to the activities that it is destined to fulfill.

Rashi, Bereishis 14:14

Although we typically translate "education" as a pedagogical process of teaching and learning new material, the Torah approach provides a much deeper understanding. The Torah-meaning of "education" is not simply instruction, but the initiation and commencement of activities that one wants to master. This is strikingly similar to the psychological concept of "scaffolding," which renowned developmental psychologist Lev Vygotsky elucidated in his theory of childhood development. According to Vygotsky, children should not only study intellectually, but should also be behaviorally instructed in specific skills at each developmental stage in order to achieve ultimate progress.[23] Scaffolding refers to continually adjusting the level of behavioral acquisition such that it is precisely just above the level that a child can

---

23 L. E. Berk and A. Winsler, *Scaffolding Children's Learning: Vygotsky and Early Childhood Education. NAEYC Research into Practice Series*, vol. 7 (Washington, DC: National Association for the Education of Young Children, 1995).

accomplish independently, but not too challenging such that they require significant support or assistance. The purpose of scaffolding is to initiate a lifelong process of independent learning. Therefore, the fundamentals of education require nothing more than (1) determining the goal of mastery (i.e., the craft with which one is destined to fulfill), and (2) providing sufficient opportunities to initiate and engage in tasks related to the goal with assistance that is progressively decreased until mastery is achieved.

Chapter 7

SPIRITUALITY

and

MENTAL HEALTH

1. A TORAH PERSPECTIVE ON TRAGEDY HELPS TO FIND VALUE IN SUFFERING

> כיון שהגיעו להר הבית ראו שועל שיצא מבית קדשי הקדשים התחילו
> הן בוכין, ור"ע מצחק. אמרו לו מפני מה אתה מצחק? אמר להם מפני
> מה אתם בוכים? אמרו לו מקום שכתוב בו (במדבר א, נא) והזר הקרב
> יומת ועכשיו שועלים הלכו בו ולא נבכה. אמר להן לכך אני מצחק...תלה
> הכתוב נבואתו של זכריה בנבואתו של אוריה...עכשיו שנתקיימה
> נבואתו של אוריה בידוע שנבואתו של זכריה מתקיימת בלשון הזה
> אמרו לו עקיבא ניחמתנו עקיבא ניחמתנו.

When a group of rabbis saw foxes scampering in the ruins of the Kodesh Hakodashim (Holy of Holies) on the Temple Mount, they began to cry, but Rabbi Akiva laughed. They asked each other to explain. The rabbis

> said, "How can we not cry when there are foxes in the holiest site, where even humans could not enter?" Rabbi Akiva explained, "The prophecy of the redemption is dependent on the prophecy of destruction. Now that the destruction has come to pass, I know that the prophecy of redemption will be fulfilled as well." The other rabbis exclaimed, "Akiva, you have comforted us! Akiva, you have comforted us!"
>
> *Talmud Bavli, Makkos* 24b

This famous Talmudic story is often cited as an example of the Jewish response to tragedy and suffering. The resiliency of the Jewish People is grounded in the holy words of the prophets who repeatedly warned of impending doom while simultaneously instilling hope in God's ultimate redemption, which is necessarily predicated by tragedy. This narrative reflects the fluctuations in the fortunes of the individual as well—perhaps best illustrated in Viktor Frankl's Logotherapy. While experiencing unimaginable human suffering at the hands of the Nazis in the Holocaust, Frankl, a psychologist, developed a defiantly positive attitude that helped him survive both physically and psychologically. His approach is summed up poignantly in one sentence: "Everything can be taken from a man but one thing: the last of the human freedoms—to choose one's attitude in any given set of circumstances."[1] Logotherapy preaches that although we cannot always control our circumstances, we have the ability and imperative to choose our perspective and how we respond. We can cry or we can laugh, and we can choose to do good. "When we are no longer able to change a situation, we are challenged to change ourselves."[2]

2. GOING TO SYNAGOGUE MAY LEAD TO A LONGER, HEALTHIER LIFE

כדאמר ר' יהושע בן לוי לבניה קדימו וחשיכו ועיילו לבי כנישתא כי היכי דתורכו חיי א"ר אחא ברבי חנינא מאי קרא (משלי ח, לד) אשרי אדם שומע לי לשקד על דלתותי יום יום לשמור מזוזת פתחי וכתיב בתריה כי מוצאי מצא חיים.

As Rabbi Yehoshua ben Levi would say to his sons: Arrive early and stay late in the synagogue, so that your lives will be lengthened. Rabbi Acha, son of Rabbi Chanina, provided a source: "Happy is the man who listens to Me, watching daily at My gates, guarding My door posts" (Mishlei 8:34). And the following verse states: "For he who finds Me finds life and obtains the favor of God" (ibid., v. 35).

Talmud Bavli, Berachos 8a

---

1 V. Frankl, *Man's Search for Meaning* (Beacon Press, 2006).
2 Ibid.

This source teaches that regularly attending synagogue can add years to one's life. Interestingly, a significant body of scientific research has supported the empirical validity of this ancient teaching. Across different religions, weekly attendance of religious services is associated with greater longevity and health.[3] Many theories have been proposed to explain this phenomenon. Most experts agree that the social support and opportunities provided by attending public prayer services are key contributors toward extending the lifespan,[4] since social interaction is one of the strongest predictors of life expectancy.[5] However, some studies have still found benefits of attending services even after controlling for levels of social support.[6] Either way, it is particularly recommended that older

---

3   P. La Cour, K. Avlund, and K. Schultz-Larsen, "Religion and Survival in a Secular Region: A Twenty-Year Follow-Up of 734 Danish Adults Born in 1914," *Social Science and Medicine* 62(1) (2006): 157–164. Also L. H. Powell, L. Shahabi, and C. E. Thoresen, "Religion and Spirituality: Linkages to Physical Health," *American Psychologist* 58(1) (2003): 36.

4   L. F. Berkman, T. Glass, I. Brissette, and T. E. Seeman, "From Social Integration to Health: Durkheim in the New Millennium," *Social Science and Medicine* 51(6) (2000): 843-857. Also D. H. Jaffe, Z. Eisenbach, Y. D. Neumark, and O. Manor, "Does Living in a Religiously Affiliated Neighborhood Lower Mortality? *Annals of Epidemiology* 15(10) (2005): 804–810.

5   L. Mineo, "Harvard study, almost 80 years old, has proved that embracing community helps us live longer and be happier," *The Harvard Gazette*, April 11, 2017.

6   E. Schnall, S. Wassertheil-Smoller, C. Swencionis, V. Zemon, L. Tinker, M. J. O'Sullivan,…and M. Goodwin, "The Relationship between Religion

adults—especially those who suffer from depression, anxiety, or physical ailments—maintain social activity and community attachment. To that end, regular attendance at a house of worship is a proven method to help accomplish that goal.

3. PRACTICING GRATITUDE IMPROVES HAPPINESS, SATISFACTION, AND MORE

> משרשי מצוה זו, שראוי לו לאדם שיכיר ויגמול חסד למי שעשה עמו טובה, ולא יהיה נבל ומתנכר וכפוי טובה שזו מדה רעה ומאוסה בתכלית לפני אלקים ואנשים.

The principle of this mitzvah (of honoring one's parents) is that it is proper for a person to recognize and show gratitude to people who were good to him, and not to be ungrateful, because that is a bad and the most repulsive attribute before God and people.

Sefer Hachinuch, mitzvah 33

Gratitude is a core value in Judaism. In fact, the etymology of the word "Judaism" is from the name Judah—son of Jacob and Leah, whose name means "gratitude."[7] Jewish prayer and practice is replete with opportunities to express gratitude to God. For instance, the first words we utter in

---

and Cardiovascular Outcomes and All-Cause Mortality in the Women's Health Initiative Observational Study," *Psychology and Health* 25(2) (2010): 249–263.

7   See *Talmud Bavli, Berachos* 7b.

the morning are "מודה אני לפניך—I give thanks to You," in acknowledgment of our gratitude for being alive for a new day. This may explain why research shows that greater levels of gratitude are closely associated with positive religious traits, such as elevated levels of belief,[8] attendance of services,[9] and engagement in prayer.[10] Practicing gratitude regularly in the form of listing things to be grateful for or verbally thanking others has incredibly positive effects. With regard to mental health research, studies on gratitude exercises found that they can reduce depression, worry, and body dissatisfaction and even improve quantity and quality of sleep.[11]

---

8   P. C. Watkins, K. Woodward, T. Stone, and R. L. Kolts, "Gratitude and Happiness: Development of a Measure of Gratitude, and Relationships with Subjective Well-Being," *Social Behavior and Personality: An International Journal* 31(5) (2003): 431–451.

9   M. G. Adler and N. S. Fagley, "Appreciation: Individual Differences in Finding Value and Meaning as a Unique Predictor of Subjective Well-Being," *Journal of Personality* 73(1) (2005): 79–114.

10 N. M. Lambert, F. D. Fincham, S. R. Braithwaite, S. M. Graham, and S. R. Beach, "Can Prayer Increase Gratitude?" *Psychology of Religion and Spirituality* 1(3) (2009): 139.

11 R. A. Emmons and M. E. McCullough, "Counting Blessings versus Burdens: An Experimental Investigation of Gratitude and Subjective Well-Being in Daily Life," *Journal of Personality and Social Psychology* 84(2) (2003): 377; A. W. Geraghty, A. M. Wood, and M. E. Hyland, "Dissociating the Facets of Hope: Agency and Pathways Predict Dropout from Unguided Self-Help Therapy in Opposite Directions," *Journal of Research in Personality* 44(1) (2010): 155–158; A. W. Geraghty, A. M. Wood, and M. E. Hyland, "Attrition from Self-Directed Interventions: Investigating the Relationship between

4. CHANGE YOUR NATURE THROUGH DAILY PRACTICE

כשיתן האדם למי שראוי אלף זהובים בבת אחת לאיש אחד ולאיש אחר
לא נתן כלום, לא יעלה בידו מידת הנדיבות בזה המעשה האחד הגדול כמו
שמגיע למי שהתנדב אלף זהובים באלף פעמים ונתן כל זהוב מהם על צד
הנדיבות, מפני שזה כפל מעשה הנדיבות אלף פעמים והגיע לו קנין חזק.

If a person gives a thousand gold coins all at once to one pauper and he gives nothing to another, he will not develop a generous nature as much as when he willingly gives a thousand gold pieces on a thousand separate occasions. This is because repeating an act of generosity a thousand times helps it become ingrained.

Rambam's commentary to *Pirkei Avos* 3:15

Here, the *Rambam* describes a fundamental principle of human behavior as observed by modern psychological science: in developing a certain personality trait, *frequency* is more powerful than *intensity*. We are creatures of habit, and it is hard to break out of ingrained patterns. Therefore, when forming good habits, it is generally more effective to engage consistently in small activities than to exert oneself intensely for a shorter

---

Psychological Predictors, Intervention Content and Dropout from a Body Dissatisfaction Intervention," *Social Science and Medicine* 71(1) (2010): 30–37; R. A. Emmons and M. E. McCullough, "Counting Blessings versus Burdens: An Experimental Investigation of Gratitude and Subjective Well-Being in Daily Life," *Journal of Personality and Social Psychology* 84(2) (2003): 377. Citations listed in consecutive order.

period of time.[12] Conversely, in reference to bad habits such as addictions, occasional slip-ups—even if they are briefly intense—are less problematic than frequent, lesser shortfalls. The excerpt above teaches us that this is also true for personality traits. While a single event or behavioral shift can lead to increases in motivation to change one's behavior, such changes tend to fade in the absence of repeated practice.[13] Virtually all effective forms of psychotherapy take this approach: they incorporate repeated and gradual application of newly acquired skills over a protracted period of time.[14] Without this essential component, change is simply not possible.

5. TAKING IT ONE STEP AT A TIME TO CHANGE YOUR LIFE

וכך היה מונה, אחת, אחת ואחת, אחת ושתים, אחת ושלש...

This is how he (the Kohen Gadol) would count: One, one and one, one and two, one and three...

Mishnah, Yoma 5:3

---

[12] K. A. Ericsson, R. T. Krampe, and C. Tesch-Römer, "The Role of Deliberate Practice in the Acquisition of Expert Performance," *Psychological Review* 100(3) (1993): 363.

[13] W. R. Miller and K. A. Mount, "A Small Study of Training in Motivational Interviewing: Does One Workshop Change Clinician and Client Behavior?" *Behavioural and Cognitive Psychotherapy* 29(4) (2001): 457–471.

[14] D. Meichenbaum, *The Evolution of Cognitive Behavior Therapy: A Personal and Professional Journey with Don Meichenbaum* (2017), 101.

The source above explains how the Kohen Gadol (High Priest) counted while performing the sprinkling ritual of a sacrifice during the Yom Kippur service—the day in the Jewish calendar most focused on repentance and positive change. The counting method is peculiar: instead of counting regularly from one to two to three, etc., the Kohen Gadol counts by repetition of "one" before each subsequent number, saying, "one and one, one and two, one and three…" Although there was a practical purpose for counting this way, there is also a deeper message that can be derived from this counting method. Once a person is inspired to change, contemplating all the steps necessary to achieve one's spiritual goals often becomes overwhelming—and the first step is often the most difficult. The Kohen Gadol's approach teaches us to be patient with our progress and take no more than one step at a time. After taking that crucial first step toward recovery, the next steps become infinitely closer. It is just "one" and then "one more." Furthermore, after each subsequent step, one should reflect and appreciate how far they have already come. In this vein, the most widely practiced treatment for addiction, the 12-Step programs, emphasize the importance of taking things "one day at a time" and also recognizing that former addicts remain vulnerable to relapse even after they have taken steps to overcome their problem.[15]

---

15 Alcoholics Anonymous (2014), *Alcoholics Anonymous: Big Book Reference Edition for Addiction Treatment.*

6. HARDSHIP CAN INCREASE OUR WILLPOWER

וְזָכַרְתָּ אֶת כָּל הַדֶּרֶךְ אֲשֶׁר הוֹלִיכְךָ ה' אֱלֹקֶיךָ זֶה אַרְבָּעִים שָׁנָה בַּמִּדְבָּר לְמַעַן עַנֹּתְךָ...וַיְעַנְּךָ וַיַּרְעִבֶךָ וַיַּאֲכִלְךָ אֶת הַמָּן אֲשֶׁר לֹא יָדַעְתָּ.

Remember the entire way that Hashem, your God made you travel in the wilderness these past forty years, in order to afflict you by hardships…He subjected you to the hardship of hunger and then gave you mann to eat that you did not know.

Devarim 8:2–3

Why would God subject the Jewish People to years of suffering in the desert? Why would He make them hungry before giving them *mann* to eat? At face value, these seem like cruel punishments unbecoming of a merciful, loving God, but perhaps a deeper understanding reflects His compassion for the Jewish People. In one famous psychology experiment, professor Roy Baumeister divided a group of college students into two rooms and assigned them the task of solving nearly impossible puzzles. In each room, he placed on the tables a plate of freshly baked chocolate chip cookies as well as a bowl of radishes. However, he only told the students in Room 1 that they were allowed to eat the cookies. The students in Room 2 were told that they were allowed to eat the radishes but *not* the cookies. He then timed how long each group worked on their respective puzzles before giving up. What happened? The students in Room 1 worked for an average of twenty minutes, whereas the students in Room 2 worked for an average of just eight minutes, even though they were completing the exact same puzzles! Baumeister concluded that the students in Room 2 had to exert more willpower by resisting the urge to eat the cookies, and they therefore "ran out of gas" more quickly.[16] Baumeister discovered in later research that withstanding hardship can gradually increase willpower over time, in much the same way that exercising a muscle through repeated exertion makes it stronger.[17] So perhaps the reason that God afflicted the Jewish People in the desert was to bolster their willpower and increase their spiritual strength. Perhaps this is the same reason why He presents us with challenges today.

7. THE ABILITY TO DELAY GRATIFICATION LEADS TO A BETTER LIFE

> וְיָצָא הָעָם וְלָקְטוּ דְּבַר יוֹם בְּיוֹמוֹ לְמַעַן אֲנַסֶּנּוּ הֲיֵלֵךְ בְּתוֹרָתִי אִם לֹא.
> **רש"י**: דְּבַר יוֹם בְּיוֹמוֹ. צרך אכילת יום ילקטו ביומו ולא היום לצרך מחר.

And the people shall go out and collect the mann they need each day, in order to test them if they will follow

---

16 R. F. Baumeister, E. Bratslavsky, M. Muraven, and D. M. Tice, "Ego Depletion: Is the Active Self a Limited Resource?" *Journal of Personality and Social Psychology* 74(5) (1998): 1252.

17 M. Muraven and R. F. Baumeister, "Self-Regulation and Depletion of Limited Resources: Does Self-Control Resemble a Muscle?" *Psychological Bulletin* 126(2) (2000): 247.

> *my Torah or not."* **Rashi:** *They may only collect what they need to eat that day, but not take extra for the next day.*
>
> *Shemos 16:4*

Many commentators point out that the "test" of the *mann* was one of self-control and trust in God.[18] Not only were the Jewish People commanded to take only what they needed for that day, but on Fridays they received a double portion because no *mann* was delivered on Shabbos. This tested their trust in God that He would provide for them each day. This situation also strengthened their self-control, especially on Fridays when they had to save a second portion for the following day. Hashem sometimes places the Jewish People in challenging situations in order to help them develop character. The ability to delay immediate gratification is associated with greater competence and success later in life. This was famously demonstrated by the Stanford Marshmallow Experiment, in which nursery age children were presented with a marshmallow and told that they could either eat the marshmallow immediately or wait several minutes and receive two marshmallows.[19] In follow-up studies many years

---

18   E.g., *Rashi, Ramban, Ibn Ezra, Abarbanel* ad loc.
19   W. Mischel, E. B. Ebbesen, and A. Raskoff Zeiss, "Cognitive and Attentional Mechanisms in Delay of Gratification," *Journal of Personality and Social Psychology* 21(2) (1972): 204.

later, those children that were able to wait were more likely to have achieved greater academic success.[20] Later research on this paradigm revealed that the perceived trustworthiness of the experimenter affected the children's willingness to delay gratification.[21] Children who trusted that the adult would follow through on the promise of greater reward were more willing to delay gratification.

8. NOTICING CHANGES IN OUR ENVIRONMENT

אף על פי שתקיעת שופר בראש השנה גזרת הכתוב, רמז יש בו כלומר עורו ישנים משנתכם ונרדמים הקיצו מתרדמתכם וחפשו במעשיכם וחזרו בתשובה וזכרו בוראכם.

Although blowing the shofar on Rosh Hashanah is a Divine decree, it also serves a practical purpose. It is as if the sound of the shofar says, "Wake up sleepers from your sleep, and those who slumber, arise from your slumber. Inspect your deeds, repent, remember your Creator."

Mishneh Torah, Hilchos Teshuvah 3:4

---

20 Y. Shoda, W. Mischel, and P. K. Peake, "Predicting Adolescent Cognitive and Self-Regulatory Competencies from Preschool Delay of Gratification: Identifying Diagnostic Conditions," *Developmental Psychology* 26(6) (1990): 978.

21 C. Kidd, H. Palmeri, and R. N. Aslin, "Rational Snacking: Young Children's Decision-Making on the Marshmallow Task Is Moderated by Beliefs about Environmental Reliability," *Cognition* 126(1) (2013): 109–114.

If you ever lived in a busy urban area, you have probably awoken to the sound of a car alarm in the middle of the night. Car alarms are designed to cycle through many different sounds to make them hard to ignore. Experiments in cognitive psychology have found that the human brain is naturally more receptive to environmental changes than constancy.[22] This is because we are faced with a constant barrage of stimuli, so Hashem bestows the ability to notice contrasts and differences so that we can efficiently process our surroundings. In this way, the shofar blasts we hear on Rosh Hashanah are truly the best type of alarm clock! We cycle through short, medium and long staccato blasts (similar to a car alarm), in order to "wake us from our slumber," just as the *Rambam* describes. Meaning that the changing sounds of the shofar have the ability to draw our attention in and get us to focus on the mission of the day—*teshuvah*. The pattern of shofar blasts cycles through various sounds, making it harder to ignore and thus more likely that we will "hear the call" to change ourselves. Interestingly, the High Holiday season resembles this pattern as well, with the disruptions to our weekly schedule and routines, and *chagim* with different, albeit complementary, spiritual foundations.

---

22 J. Downar, A. P. Crawley, D. J. Mikulis, and K. D. Davis, "A Multimodal Cortical Network for the Detection of Changes in the Sensory Environment," *Nature Neuroscience* 3(3) (2000).

On a visual level, the Jewish calendar in the month of Tishrei almost resembles a Morse code representation of the shofar sounds—two days of *yom tov*/ several days of *chol*/ *yom tov*/ several days of *chol*, followed by *yom tov*/ *chol hamoed*/ *yom tov* again. Perhaps the on-again-off-again schedule of our lives is designed to shake up our lives, throw us out of our routine a bit and inspire us to make changes.

9. GUIDED IMAGERY AND VISUALIZATIONS CAN HELP US FULFILL OUR POTENTIAL

הציור הוא המפתח לאמונה. ציורים מעוררים ומחזקים את הכח, והם המבססים את המחשבה.

Visualization is the key to faith. Visualizations awaken, strengthen the will, and are the foundation of thought.
Rabbi Shomo Wolbe, *Alei Shur*, vol. 1, p. 104

This source emphasizes how utilizing imaginative visualizations can strengthen our convictions, influence our mental and emotional states, and improve our ability to achieve our goals in life. Over the past thirty years, psychological science has examined and studied how this process works. First, the human mind is so powerful that when we conjure up vivid images, we can actually fool our brain into reacting as if they are real. This can have both positive and negative consequences on our functionality and well-being. On the one hand, we can teach ourselves to visualize in a way that enhances creativity and performance,[23] but on the other hand, we can get stuck in thoughts about negative experiences (e.g., it is common for individuals with Posttraumatic Stress Disorder to reexperience traumas of the past long after the events occurred).[24] When we visualize, our motor and sensory neural networks fire in the same way as they do when we are confronted with actual stimuli.[25] For these reasons, as Rav Wolbe suggests, guided imagery can be an effective treatment strategy that can yield beneficial therapeutic effects. Specifically, conjuring up positive scenarios in our mind's eye about our future can make it more likely for them to become reality. For instance, studies in sports psychology have found that coaching athletes to imagine a successful foul shot, tennis serve, golf putt, or penalty kick

---

23 M. Louridas, E. M. Bonrath, D. A. Sinclair, N. J. Dedy, and T. P. Grantcharov, "Randomized Clinical Trial to Evaluate Mental Practice in Enhancing Advanced Laparoscopic Surgical Performance," *British Journal of Surgery* 102(1) (2015): 37–44.

24 L. Jelinek, S. Randjbar, M. Kellner, A. Untiedt, J. Volkert, C. Muhtz, and S. Moritz, "Intrusive Memories and Modality-Specific Mental Imagery in Posttraumatic Stress Disorder," *Zeitschrift für Psychologie/Journal of Psychology* 218 (2015): 64–70.

25 J. Pearson, T. Naselaris, E. A. Holmes, and S. M. Kosslyn, "Mental Imagery: Functional Mechanisms and Clinical Applications," *Trends in Cognitive Sciences* 19(10) (2015): 590–602.

actually reduces performance anxiety and thereby improves technique.[26]

Credits: Rabbi Ben Geiger, Los Angeles, CA

10. CHARACTER CHANGE IS THE GREATEST HUMAN ACHIEVEMENT

The loudest sound in the universe is the breaking of a bad habit.

...

It is more difficult to change a single character trait than to learn the entire Talmud.[27]

Rabbi Yisrael Salanter

When people struggle to beat a bad habit or overcome a problematic personality trait, it is often difficult to appreciate small changes. These famous quotations convey the Torah perspective that changing internalized patterns of thought, feeling, and behavior is the most challenging thing in the universe, but also the most impactful. This being the case,

---

26 R. C. Thelwell and I. A. Greenlees, "Developing Competitive Endurance Performance Using Mental Skills Training," *The Sport Psychologist* 17(3) (2003): 318–337.

27 As quoted in D. Katz, *The Mussar Movement*, vol. 1, pt. 1 (Tel Aviv: Orly Press, 1977), p. 120.

even the smallest of changes is an enormous accomplishment that makes a "loud sound" both in the heavens and on earth.

11. THE ULTIMATE CURE FOR IMPROVING ONE'S CHARACTER

רפאות המידות אינה בסמים גשמים, וכשם שהחלי איננו גוף, כך רפואתו
אינה מן הגופים. החלי הוא הרגש נפשי, והרפואה—הרגש נפשי.

The cure for bad character traits is not by way of medications; the disease is not one of the body and therefore its cure is not a material substance. The disease is of a person's inner nature and the cure is also that.

Chazon Ish, *Emunah U'Bitachon* 4:14

In this source, the Chazon Ish explains the limits of pharmacotherapy (medication) as a psychological intervention, and conveys that ultimately the refinement of character and regulation of emotions involves nothing more or less than a deeply spiritual process of behavior change. There is certainly a utility and place for medication in modern psychiatry. Some individuals are too distressed to engage in the process of psychotherapy, and need a lift or a decrease in distress to make it possible to change. However, clinical science has clearly revealed many substantive limitations of the use of medication as a primary or sole intervention. It is particularly interesting that the incidence and severity of mental disorders have increased manyfold throughout Western society since the advent and widespread promulgation of psychiatric medications, as has the frequency of self-injury and suicidal behavior. Furthermore, and more centrally, anti-depressants, anxiolytics, stimulants, mood stabilizers and the like can alleviate some suffering in many cases, but they cannot provide human beings with a sense of meaning, purpose, fulfillment, or happiness. For that, we must use spirituality to develop our characters and refine our day-to-day behaviors.

ABOUT THE AUTHORS

DAVID H. ROSMARIN, PHD, ABPP, is an assistant professor in the Department of Psychiatry at Harvard Medical School and director of the McLean Hospital Spirituality and Mental Health Program. He is also the founder and director of the Center for Anxiety, which has offices in Manhattan, Brooklyn, and Monsey.

RABBI SAUL HAIMOFF, PSYD, was a postdoctoral fellow at the Center for Anxiety during authorship of this book. He is now a licensed clinical psychologist, head rabbi of the Brandeis School, and an associate rabbi at the Jewish Center of Atlantic Beach.